Chiara Lubich

A Life for Unity

An Interview by Franca Zambonini

Chiara Lubich

A Life for Unity

New City

London   Edinburgh   Dublin   New York

Published in Great Britain and the United States by
New City, 57 Twyford Ave., London W3 9PZ and
New City Press, 86 Mayflower Ave., New Rochelle, NY 10801
©1992 New City, London

Translated by Margaret Coen from the original Italian
L'avventura dell'Unità
©1991 Edizioni Paoline

British Library Cataloguing in Publication Data:

Zambonini, Franca
 Chiara Lubich: Life for Unity
 I. Title   II. Coen, Margaret
 270.82092

ISBN 0-904287-45-9

Printed in the United States of America

Contents

Introduction

Global Perspectives

In the vast Sacred Hall in Tokyo, ten thousand Japanese listen to Chiara Lubich share the story of her spiritual journey while ten video monitors relay the event to the foyer and corridors outside which are packed with the overflow from the hall. It is 28 December 1981 and the first time someone from the West who is both lay and Catholic has addressed such an assembly of Buddhists. Only a few years earlier it would have been difficult to imagine a similar event taking place.

'I have only to say: "Greet Chiara", and everybody understands', said Pope John Paul II to an international gathering of twenty thousand young people at the Paleur, on 31 March 1990. On that occasion, the speeches of both the Pope and Chiara were transmitted live to all five continents through the Olympus satellite in a spectacular global encounter. In Hong Kong it was 11 p.m., in Melbourne it was 3 a.m., in Los Angeles, it was 5 a.m., and everywhere, there were hundreds of thousands, perhaps millions watching. During the Gulf War, a prayer chain launched by Chiara spurred 1.5 million people to stop working for a few minutes at midday and unite in praying for peace.

It is not easy to understand why this Movement founded by Chiara Lubich has had such a profound effect on people. Cardinal Ugo Poletti suggested his own explanation at a meeting for Focolarini in Rome on 27 May 1990. He said: 'At home as a boy in Piedmont, a region that abounds in those ancient oak trees, renowned for their hard wood, I remember being amazed at the countless blows it took to hammer a nail into one of those gnarled trunks but once you had knocked it in, no one could ever get it out again. And this is what I think the Focolare Movement has done. They speak of unity, of union, of a spirituality of unity, of mutual love as the foundation of a new world. You hear these ideas over and over again until they become lodged in people's hearts like the nail you cannot extract from the oak.'

A Tree with Twenty-Two Branches

Of the movements that have emerged in Italy during this century, the Focolare Movement or 'Work of Mary' whose foundress and president is Chiara Lubich, is alone in having had a worldwide expansion with more than 80,000 internal members, 1.5 million adherents and several million friends of the Movement present in some 156 nations.

It was while the city of Trent was being devastated in the bombing of the last war that the Movement came to life. Its growth was unforeseen and not based on any formal plan. Its strength and importance evolved gradually, in stages, enabling it to develop a complex structure without losing its early simplicity.

'A tree that has become both luxuriant and fruitful', is how Pope John Paul II described the Movement, and it does resemble a tree, a tree with twenty-two different branches.

The description 'new' has always accompanied each nascent branch of the Movement so there is 'New Generation', 'New Families', 'New Humanity' and so on. 'New' also was the inspiration that led to the foundation of the Movement as well as the ideas that have continued to emerge throughout the Movement's history. The Focolare Movement, founded by lay people, restored status and importance to the laity at a time when Church structures only afforded the faithful, whether they were youth, couples, mothers and fathers of families or whoever, a right to a place in the pew on Sundays and little else. But in addition to this, the Movement has worked in renewing unity among Catholics, in seeking unity with Christians of other denominations and in opening up dialogue with believers of other faiths as well as with non-believers—and all long before the ecumenical commitment that emerged from the Second Vatican Council.

Although the Movement has a vast international influence and its projects respond to the needs of the world today, it has a low media profile. In television jargon you would say: 'It doesn't make a good story'. The television camera ignores it, and reporters and journalists look elsewhere. This curious lack of a public image is due in part to the discreet and unobtrusive style of the Focolarini and in part to the media's indifference to the spiritual arena.

When the Italian national television news presenter announced on 28 February 1977 that the Templeton Prize for 'Progress in Religion' had been awarded to the Italian Chiara Lubich, foundress of the Focolare Movement, most viewers would have wondered who on earth this Chiara Lubich was. They would have gathered that she must be well known as soon as the announcer explained that the Templeton Prize, founded in 1972, had previously been awarded to Mother Teresa of Calcutta, Roger Schutz, the Prior of Taizé, the ex-President of India, Radhakrishnan and to Cardinal Leo-Josef Suenens.

The Charism

Chiara Lubich was born in Trent on 22 January 1920. Her surname is a throwback to the 'Middle Europe' of the Hapsburg Empire. Her early life had nothing to distinguish it from that of her peers except in that she possessed a certain indefinable eagerness of spirit. Until 1939, that is, when at the age of nineteen she visited Loreto to take part in a Catholic Students' rally.

'It was there', writes Enzo Maria Fondi, a Focolarino and someone who works closely with her, 'within the walls of the Holy House darkened with age, in silence and unexpectedly, as so often happens with the things of God, that Chiara encountered her charism for the first time. . . . But this was just the beginning, a preparation for what was to happen as she understood with clarity and certitude that a new way was opening up before her and before all who would follow her. Although she did not fully understand yet the complete meaning of this calling, she nevertheless experienced a deep certainty and joy and those elements, the DNA you might say, of what was to be the future movement'.

Three Special Dates

Three dates spanning five years have a special significance for the Movement. The first is 7 December 1943, the day on which Chiara offered her life to God in a private chapel service. This personal gift of her whole life to God is regarded as the 'birth certificate' of the Movement which will celebrate its first half century on 7 December 1993. The second is 13 May 1944. Trent had suffered severe bombing in a series of attacks from the 'Flying Fortresses' which had left the city in ruins. The Lubichs' house was hit and the family was forced to flee. Chiara, however, decided to stay on in Trent to be near her new companions. This decision was clearly an important one. Chiara herself did not yet know what the future would hold but whatever it would be, she had chosen to go with it and be faithful to it forever. The third date is 13 September 1948 when Chiara met Igino Giordani. Giordani, the controversial writer and journalist, one-time target of the fascists and friend and mentor of post-war Catholic youth, such as Giorgio la Pira and don Primo Mazzolari, had recently been elected to Parliament.

Writings of Giordani airing his complaints at the poor status accorded to the laity, for instance: 'There's not one married person in the calendar of saints' or 'We lay people only get the crumbs; we're like a spiritual proletariat', explain why Chiara's prophetic vision appealed to him as it did.

This Catholic Member of Parliament was committed to working for unity among all believers whatever their denomination. He referred to this goal as 'a longing you feel in the air, but not in the Church'. His contribution to the Focolare was to be an extraordinary one and immensely fruitful, to the extent that Chiara describes him as 'co-founder' of the Movement.

A United World

It is not easy to sum up a Movement as complex and yet as simple as this one. Both the Focolarini of the original founding group and later generations recall their mothers and fathers being upset by their decision to enter the Focolare and how their parents would ask over and over again: 'But what is this Movement all about?' In fact, the first parent asking this question was Chiara's own father, Luigi Lubich.

But perhaps the Movement was most clearly described by Pope John Paul II. At Genfest '90 (a festival of Young People for a United World, one of the 22 Focolare branches), the Pope said: 'The prospect of a united world is the hope of today's world ... to go towards a civilization which reveals itself as a true civilization of love. Clearly, an ideal such as this cannot come about by chance'.

Almost fifty years earlier, in the gloom of the shelters and the terror of war, this same prophet-like inspiration had spurred the young schoolteacher from Trent to nurture a hope barely conceivable in her day, if not in God's providential plans, and yet one that much later would come to be recognized as a veritable sign of the times.

'We are like a small hand helping the Church to carry out Jesus' wish: "that all may be one" '. This is how Chiara presented her Work to Pope John Paul II when he visited the Focolare headquarters at Rocca di Papa to get to know them better.

And six years later the Pope granted a unique privilege to Chiara in approving the Movement's statutes which stipulate that the president of the Work of Mary should always be a woman.

Hidden as We Are

Chiara Lubich bears her seventy years gracefully and has retained the energy and freshness of the early days of the Movement. When she speaks in the gentle Trentine accent which she has never lost, you are struck by the extraordinary depth of her spirituality, a spirituality whose spontaneity and straightforwardness has enabled her to move easily among the great religious leaders of our time, among young people from all over the world, along the corridors of the Vatican and in the slums of Recife. Chiara's own person reflects this spirituality with her perfectly groomed silver hair, her discreet elegance of dress, her ready smile and her unfailingly pleasant manner and the clarity with which she communicates complex insights.

Chiara lives in the geographical heart of the Movement, the International Centre of the Focolare at Rocca di Papa near Rome and as she herself says: 'camouflaged in the world, hidden because our vocation is to be immersed in the world'. She enjoys little public exposure other than the large meetings with her Focolarini and is uncomfortable talking about herself.

We are indebted to her for her total availability despite her natural, innate reluctance.

F.Z.

I

A New Spirit

The Gospel Rediscovered

The first time the Pope visited the Focolare headquarters at Rocca di Papa, your thoughts Chiara, returned, as you confided later, to the early days of the Movement. You said, 'In my mind's eye were those early days, when the Movement was coming to life and I was fascinated by this new ideal and my father used to ask, "But what is this ideal, my girl? What is this ideal?" And I would say, "It's love, dad, it's love." We did not know how else to describe it.' How would you reply today to that question your father asked you about half a century ago?

When the Pope visited us on that occasion, he referred to 'the Movement's spark of inspiration', and that is exactly what we experienced when we started living this new life with its extraordinary rediscovery of God as love and our divine birthright as his children. We understood that we had to become like him, to become love. That's why my thoughts returned that day to the reply I gave to my father.

Even now this same supernatural love is the very soul and foundation of our life, as indeed it is for Christianity itself. Then, as the Movement started to take shape, this love began to emerge as a spirituality, the spirituality of unity based on the main truths of our faith, although it also has a distinct identity of its own. It is this rich spirituality which is the motivating force of the Movement.

What is new in the Focolare Movement's contribution to the Church?

Although we now have almost half a century of experience, it is difficult, if not impossible, to measure its specific contribution to the Church. Many speak of a 'new spirit', of a 'new atmosphere' which comes about wherever people are trying to live this full evangelical communion according to the main points of our spirituality. I could say that, insofar as the Movement has lived up to its vocation, it may have reinforced the desire for unity in the Church, as well as enhanced an awareness of the need for the Church's various institutions to act together in a spirit of communion and co-operation.

But no one is really in a position to evaluate the importance and fruitfulness of what the Holy Spirit has done and continues to do through a charism that comes from him, despite having been entrusted to fragile vessels and weak instruments.

The Wide Net

Would you agree that the Gospel is a richer source of inspiration and more complete in itself than any one way of living it out?

15

I believe that the main ideas or guidelines of a spirituality can only be interpreted and lived out in the context of the whole Gospel and all that is connected with the Gospel. To see it in any other way is to detract from it and would be a serious mistake.

This is because the Gospel is like a wide net. It's as if by grasping twelve of its links, that is the twelve points of our spirituality, we lift up the whole net.

You could say that our spirituality rests on the twelve points that the Holy Spirit underlined for us in the Gospel, but at the same time, our spirituality is the whole of the Gospel.

I think this happened because, while the Church was to recognize the need for and to implement a very varied programme of re-evangelization, the Holy Spirit was preparing resources—and ours was among them—to maximize its effectiveness.

What are these twelve 'links'?

They are God-Love, the will of God, the love of our neighbour, the New Commandment of Jesus, unity, Jesus in our midst, Jesus crucified and forsaken, Jesus in the Eucharist, Mary, the Church and the Holy Spirit.

Shouldn't what you say apply perfectly naturally to all Christians? Do you have to be a Focolarino to live the Gospel completely?

During the first months we felt sure that what we were 'discovering' was already being lived in the Church. It was all so 'Christian', so 'evangelical' and so in tune with the Church's thinking that we couldn't have imag-

16

ined it wasn't already part of the common Christian heritage. It was only later that we realized that we were bringing something new and a way of life which was a bit out of the ordinary.

Of course, there is nothing new in what we practise, because it's just the age old truths of the Gospel. What is new is the focus and framework they provide when lived out in response to the needs of our time along the lines suggested by the Holy Spirit. Take the image of a kaleidoscope. It's as if the Holy Spirit with a master-stroke has shaken up the divine kaleidoscope of evangelical truths such as the beatitudes, the virtues, the evangelical counsels etc., and has given the world (and every charism is for everyone) these same elements but arranged in a new pattern that inspires and attracts people of today's world.

You ask whether you have to be a Focolarino to practise mutual love, unity and the presence of Jesus among us. Of course you don't, because all of this is part of our Christian identity, and you cannot say you are Christ's disciple unless you try to live these evangelical truths. But just as on other occasions in the Church's history, the Lord wanted to give the human race a bit of a hand, with the Focolare Movement he has found a way to emphasize these truths. Our experience is a modest one, a trial run, a small-scale but living model of what the whole of society could be like if everyone lived like this.

So what's the difference between a Focolarino and just an ordinary Christian?

The Focolarini are different from what you call 'just ordinary Christians' in the same way as the Franciscans, 'nicans, the Benedictines and the Jesuits are Just as you can photograph a room from ...eral perspectives, from the doorway, from the window, from the floor or from the ceiling, and yet it is always the same room you are photographing, so it is with Christianity: you can see it from a variety of angles. You can see it from the angle of poverty, for example, as do the Franciscans, or from prayer as do St Teresa of Avila and St John of the Cross, or from penance as did many of the spiritual trends in the Middle Ages, or from prayer and work as do the Benedictines. In our Movement you see Christianity from the angle of unity.

Of the movements which have emerged in Italy during this last century, the Focolare Movement is the only one to have achieved a worldwide expansion. Why is this?

I am often asked about this question, because, for someone looking at it from the outside, it is difficult to see the reason for the Movement's spreading so widely. My answer is always the same. I think there are two main reasons. The first is our unity with the Church's hierarchy with which we are in full harmony, as Jesus said, 'Whoever listens to you listens to me'.[1] In this unity with the hierarchy of the Church, which represents Christ, the head, Christians are like branches linked to the vine and so grace flows through them abundantly. The second reason is the unity among us in Christ's name, and you know it is the unity among Christians that converts the world: 'May they be one . . . that the world may believe. . .'[2]

You are a woman and head an international movement which is known throughout the world and which brings together people of every background and faith. Isn't this rather unique, maybe even strange?

I'll let St Paul answer that one. 'There is neither man nor woman, nor Greek nor Jew, nor freeman nor slave'.[3] We are all equal. When I work for the Movement I don't feel so much a woman as a disciple of Christ.

What the Chief Said

You once told the story of your meeting with the chief of the Bangwa people in Cameroon, who after hearing about the expansion of the Movement remarked, 'You are a woman and therefore worth nothing. Tell me, how did you do all this?' The chief's frankness doesn't surprise me since, even if worded rather differently, this same disbelief towards successful women is apparent in places quite different from Cameroon. What difference has your being a woman made to the Movement?

I remember that episode very well. I also remember that his remark didn't offend me in the least. I felt perfectly at ease, since I knew only too well that what I had described to that African chief wasn't the work of a woman but the work of God. And now, many years later, I'm even more convinced of that.

But I'm also aware that there must be a reason why God chose a woman for one of his Works, as, in fact, he has done in other instances too. Perhaps he wanted to point out that Mary has a role of her own in the Church, and that we cannot do without her presence, if for no other reason than that it was God himself who chose her. I think you could say that the fact that I'm a woman,

19

as well as the task that the Lord has entrusted to me, help together to bring out Mary's presence in the Church.

To add anything more would be wrong, because both my vocation as a woman and my role in the Church and the Movement, make sense only in the light of the unparalleled model of the Immaculate Mother of God and Mother of the Church.

The Last Shall Be First

So what role is there for women in the Church today?

If we are to speak of today, it's useful to recall 'yesterday'. In her day, St Teresa of Avila who was described as 'the most saintly of women and the most womanly of saints' used to ask the Lord for justice for women. She prayed: 'When I observe these times of ours, I do not find it at all just that virtuous and strong hearts are despised simply because they are in women. . . . You, Lord, are a just judge, unlike the judges of this world all of whom, being sons of Adam, and therefore men, regard every virtue a woman possesses with suspicion'.[4]

But also much closer to our own times, the little Thérèse of Lisieux had severe criticism for women's position and consoled herself with the thought: 'In heaven Jesus will make it quite clear that his thoughts are not those of men, since there, the last shall be first'.[5]

I wanted to quote these two great saints to show how things are changing. I think you could say, looking at the past, a not too distant past, that the situation today is somewhat improved.

Do you think that public opinion is sufficiently informed and objective in its attitude to the Focolare Movement? Have you ever met with prejudice?

We ran into prejudice more often in the past, when little was known about the Movement, than now. Prejudice and unfounded criticism seldom remain when people get to know the Movement better. I realize, however, how important it is to supply correct and thorough information about a Work which is both extremely simple and complex at the same time. The spirituality of the Movement can be defined quite clearly, but there are some theological implications that are not quite as easy to understand. It's easy to describe the Movement's structure and its range of branches, but it's more difficult to grasp the nature of the Movement's unity and diversity. Since the Movement shares in the Church's own nature and image, I think you have to bear in mind that it is also partner to the Church's mystery. This is, in fact, how we see it. The Movement, like the Church herself, shares in the mystery of the Holy Trinity. St Cyprian said that the universal Church is 'a people assembled by the unity of the Father, the Son and the Holy Spirit.'[6] While we have gone forward building this Movement under the guidance of the Holy Spirit, he has always set our sights on the Unity and the Trinity of God.

The Lamp on the Lampstand

How did you feel when you were awarded the Templeton Prize?

When I heard that I had been selected for the Templeton Prize, I was amazed. I thought, 'What, there's a prize for what you do in the religious field?' I had always imagined that the only reward for this was heaven and eternal life.

My second thought was, 'But the award isn't being given to me, but to God's Work. And so, "When a lamp is lit, it is not put under the bushel basket, but on a lampstand, where it gives light to everyone in the house. Like the lamp, you must shed your light among your fellows, so that, when they see the good you do, they may praise your Father in heaven." '[7] So I decided that, since I hadn't sought this award (it was a complete surprise to me), God might have a plan of his own behind it.

In fact, when I made my speech at the Guildhall in London, it seemed to me as if all of us present in that hall had come together, united as one, even though we were of different religions, and I wondered what the reason for this could be. Was it perhaps because we were all believers so that gathered together there, we were all together enfolded in his presence? Then when we went into the reception, the first to approach me were the guests of other faiths; for example a Tibetan monk who told me he wanted to write straightaway to the Dalai Lama in India so that we might be in contact with one another and then four Jewish guests came over to express their joy at the fact that the Old Testament was the trunk on to which the New Testament was grafted, as if to say, and so is the development of this whole Movement. Then Sikhs and Hindus and others came and it seemed to me that this occasion was providing the Movement with a new opening. From then on we would have to try to take our spirit, our life, not only to the other Churches or Christian communities but also to our brothers and sisters of other faiths.

How did you feel when you became famous? What were your reactions when you became a public figure and the Movement became known outside Christian circles?

Everything happened so naturally and gradually that there wasn't a problem. The very word 'fame' sounds strange. This isn't about a person, it's about God's Work.

'Tanéta e Buséta'

While on one hand, the Movement is known throughout the whole world, on the other hand, it seems to keep itself in the background. The media pays it little attention and it has a very low profile when you compare it to other groups such as Communion and Liberation which always ends up in the papers because of some controversial statement or one or other of its projects. Is what I'd describe as the 'Focolare's avoiding the limelight' a deliberate choice or is it because of a general lack of interest in Christian activities?

It's our own choice. It goes back to the early days of the Movement and we've never gone back on it in spite of this being the era of the mass media. I remember a saintly priest, who's since been beatified, saying in his local Veronese dialect, 'Tanéta e buséta', which in simple words means 'Be humble and hidden, no exhibitionism, no clatter'. It was a wise piece of advice which suited us well when the Movement, which was just coming to life might have appeared too innovative and at odds with the general religious scenario of the time. And nowadays our attitude is the same, and it seems an appropriate one for those whose aim is holiness. Of course, we don't shun modern means of communication. In fact, we use the most up-to-date audio and visual equipment within the Movement for the training of and for communication with our members. At the last Genfest, a youth event which takes place every five years at Rome's Paleur stadium, we gratefully accepted Italian national television's offer to transmit the festival on the experimental Olympus satellite. It was really providential as we would never have been able to afford the four hours of live satellite time which enabled hundreds of thousands of young people in the furthest corners of Europe and North and South America to share in the event. So we don't object to mass media, but we are convinced at the same time that personal relationships, love for our neighbour, and a living witness are more genuine means of spreading the Gospel message.

Nevertheless, isn't it true to say that while you Chiara are practically idolized within the Movement, outside of it, little is known about you?

Idolized? Certainly not, perhaps loved, in fact very much loved. The reason little is known about me outside the Movement isn't that I dislike or avoid the public. A number of biographies have been published as well as diaries and collections of spiritual thoughts which reveal the sort of person I am and what I think.

I've been speaking in public about my religious experience for over ten years now, to thousands and thousands of Christians, Buddhists and so on, in several continents, but I have to admit that I find it physically impossible to accept all the invitations, and I get dozens of them, to do interviews and address public meetings. Apart from that, it's my firm belief that our path is like that of the family of Nazareth which was known only for its industriousness and silence. Jesus himself spent thirty years in obscurity and only three preaching, scarcely ten per cent of his earthly life. If you think of Mary, the one who kept everything in her heart, I wonder how much she was concerned with the footlights and the cultivation of a public persona.

Chiara, Chiaretta, Chiarella

Many Focolarini christen their children with names like Chiara, Chiaretta and Chiarella. Does this sort of affectionate devotion bother you?

Not at all; in any case, I think my name reminds them not so much of me as a person but of a spirituality which is all light and clarity, and so I feel that gestures like these of affection or devotion are directed towards our great ideal.

Quite often when people meet you, they are impressed by your fashionable appearance. What would you say to those who expect the foundress of a Movement in the Church to be dressed, if not quite like a nun, at least in grey?

Every spirituality of a certain weight in the Church has an influence on the way its followers dress and the appearance of their homes. Think of the many humble

Franciscan churches built in wood and the tunics worn by these friars who are renowned for poverty, or think of the mighty abbeys at the heart of the rural foundations, like small scale cities, of St Benedict which exemplify his spirituality of praying and working.

The key word for us is unity and our approach to our brothers and sisters is to make ourselves one with them and one with the places where we live and work. Among the Focolarini there are those who live and work in India, in Tokyo, others in Melbourne or in the shanty towns of Brazil and the slums of Manila. There are some who work in the sophisticated offices of European cities and those who live and work among the destitute of Africa. Some work at the U.N. and others in various departments of the Vatican. While some teach in schools, others stay at home and others again work in hospitals. Some have to address public meetings or perhaps organize conferences for thousands of people of different social backgrounds. There are those who have a lot to do with religious and civil authorities. . . . Each one has to adapt to the environment and dress like those he or she meets.

Dressing Harmoniously

There is, however, a common denominator linking all the members of the Movement in that their way of dressing should be harmonious. We've always been of the opinion that since God isn't only goodness, holiness and truth but also the sum of all beauty, so we are called to witness to this aspect too, of course always with the aims of the Movement in mind. Unity itself means the highest harmony, order and beauty, and the Focolarini's Rule testifies to this. It says: 'The Focolarini will always maintain decorum and good taste, modesty and simplicity of style. They will dress according to the times so that they do not stand out from those around them. They will be conscious of their specific aim which brings them into contact with non-believers who are frequently opposed to the Church, and they will try to witness not only to the truth and goodness of Christianity but, also through their appearance, they will be an expression of harmony.' The General Statute of the Movement which regards all the members of the Movement adds: 'Their dress will reflect Jesus' words: "Consider the lilies of the field, how they grow; they neither toil nor spin; yet I tell you even Solomon in all his glory was not arrayed like one of these".'[8]

The Gospel contains certain elements which haven't yet emerged in their full splendour, but if God calls us to live them, then we must.

'You can recognize the Focolarini', said Pope Paul VI, 'from their laughter and from their smiles.' I have heard people who don't know you saying: 'What have they got to laugh about, these Focolarini?'

In his parting words, his 'testament', Jesus promises the fullness of joy. It's a gift that can often be seen on our faces. Perhaps at times, it can annoy people or even be out of place. Nevertheless, it's true that the Focolarino's uniform is his smile.

Which passage of the Gospel, which religious feast and which saint appeal to you most?

27

My, or rather, our favourite passage of the Gospel is the one which contains the testament of Jesus, that is, his words and his prayer after the last supper as in John Chapter 17.

And my favourite religious feast? I can't choose one. They are all the main feasts of the liturgical calendar.

And my favourite saint? It is the saint of saints, the Lord Jesus, crucified, risen and present among us.

II

A Schoolteacher from Trent

Chiara, we know a lot about the Movement but very little about you. What was your background like and what was your home town of Trent like when you were a child?

People know little about me. . .! Before I answer, can I just say how difficult I find this sort of question. If there is any sense in my past, or in what I am now, it's only in as much as I have been one of those useless and unfaithful instruments God uses to build a Work which is his own Work. Once a Work has been built, it's the Work you look at and not at the instrument, just as when you admire an artist's painting, you look at the picture and not at the brushes used. Christian discipline teaches us to think of God and other people, not of ourselves. This is the path I have tried to follow so I can't really see the relevance of questions like this one, but if you want me to, then of course I'll answer.

First of all, my background? Well, I was born in Trent in 1920, two years after the end of the First World War. It was a peaceful time for my family, and I remember my mother saying that this is why I inherited a calm and serene nature.

The Trent of my childhood was a little city with between forty to fifty thousand inhabitants. It grew up at the time of the Romans, in a valley sheltered by high mountains and three hills, from which it got its name 'Tridentum'. The town had a quiet, industrious and contained air about it and took pride in its few but important historical monuments like the fifteenth century Cathedral situated in one of Italy's most beautiful squares; its towers and the great Castle of Good Counsel. Then, just as now, the enduring memory of the Church Council named after the city, the Council of Trent, hovered over the town and is depicted in a famous period painting which hangs in the church of St Mary Major where I was christened Silvia.

A Socialist Father. . .

What was your family like?

My father Luigi and my mother Luigina were both working in the printing business when they met. He was a foreman and she was a typesetter at the daily newspaper, *Il Popolo*, the voice of the Trentine socialists run by Cesare Battisti whom my mother respected enormously. She used to go to morning mass daily and then on to work and her mass missal was always beside her on the work bench. I remember her saying, 'Mr Battisti has never once told me to put it away; he has always respected my faith'.

Mother was a very devout woman. As well as daily mass and communion she was also very faithful to a number of other devotions too. For sixty years—she was ninety-four when she died—she never once missed the monthly vigil in honour of Our Lady of Pompei. She was intelligent and strong-minded but also deeply sensitive. I remember how she used to sing when the financial situation of the family was stable and how she used to suffer when times were hard and it was difficult to find the money for our school fees.

Dad was a socialist and hardly a practising Catholic until his children influenced him enough to make him go back to church. Because he refused to give in to fascism, he endured poverty and hunger and all of us with him. Just after the war, he was working in the wine trade, but the economic crisis ruined the business, and he had to close it down in 1930. This was followed by long years of unemployment. Before the war he had known Mussolini, who was both a neighbour of ours as well as editor-in-chief of Battisti's newspaper. My father was frequently advised to take advantage of his acquaintance with Mussolini to get ahead, but a man such as my father who had rejected the fascist ticket was hardly likely to take up this sort of advice. I remember how when we had to dress up in our uniforms for the children's meetings on Saturdays, mother used to try and smuggle us out of the house.

He was a person who was both large of heart and large of mind. I knew that he loved me dearly and understood me.

. . . and a Communist Brother

There were four of us. Gino was the eldest and I came second, then Lilliana and Carla. We were very close as children and still are. Lilliana married a senator and they live in Trent with their five children. She has been close to the Movement since the beginning. Carla married a naval officer who's now retired. They live in

Rome and have three children. Carla and I have always been close. Gino also lives in Rome and has five children. I've got lots of nieces and nephews and grand-nieces and nephews. I get along well with them all, although obviously I'm closer to some more than others. We all gather together about twice a year, at least with those who are in Rome, and it's always a celebration.

I've always admired Gino's intelligence. Even as a child he was so generous. I remember once when we children had been misbehaving and mother was waiting for dad to come home to punish us. Dad lined us up by age, first Gino then me, next Lilliana and last Carla. We were each to get a good smack. Gino got it first, and then it was my turn, but Gino stood in front of me and said, 'Don't smack Silvia, smack me instead.'

Gino was a resistance fighter with the Garibaldi Brigade; he was a communist, but the sort of communist who had been attracted to the idea of revolution more by love for the poor and oppressed than anything else. When he used to work as a medical assistant at St Clare's Hospital, he often used to give his earnings to the poor. Later, he became a journalist and worked as co-director of the Trentine CLN *National Liberation* and then with *Unity* in Milan. After some years, Gino moved to Rome, and I think it was the events in Hungary in 1956 which brought him to a deep crisis of conscience. After this, he gave the benefit of his journalistic experience to the Movement and became a strong supporter of it. It was through Gino that our magazine, *New City*, got started, and he still works for it now.

One incident during the war is quite revealing about my brother. Trent had just suffered heavy bombing and my journey home that day was alongside wrecked buildings and uprooted trees. I stopped at St Clare's

Hospital where Gino was working. A whole wing had received a direct hit, and all its female patients had perished. As Gino pointed out the total chaos, he whispered, 'Just look, everything is vanity'. He voiced what was passing through my own mind, as if to confirm the choice I had made for my own life.

What is your earliest memory?

I remember that when I was about three or four years old, we used to go to the mountains in the summer. We slept in a mountain refuge which was full of hay and in the mornings we used to get washed in the cold spring water at the pump. After that, we children, bare to the waist, used to play to our hearts' content, sliding down the grassy slopes on wooden boards. And there, surrounded by nature, with the breeze in our faces and the thrill of the descent, I felt a happiness and freedom which I still recall to this day.

A Little Girl Called Silvia

What sort of child was Silvia? Was she outgoing or quiet, joyous or serious, impressionable or strong-minded, or none of these?

I don't know. You'd really have to ask the others. I think I was rather thoughtful and conscientious. I didn't have much time for dolls because I felt they were make-believe. I didn't like fairy-tales either; I liked true stories. Of course, I had all the usual childish faults, and mother would sometimes have to correct me because I wasn't helping her enough around the house. I tended to choose to do what I thought was more important, like studying, for example.

What were your earliest formative experiences?

The fact that my family was a closely knit one was certainly important, and the religious education I received from the Sisters of the Child Mary in Trent was also a strong influence in my upbringing.

I have lovely memories of those days. I enjoyed learning and loved hearing about the truths of our religion, which later were to be the foundation of the Movement I was called to build.

When I was ten I was seriously ill with peritonitis following appendicitis. Only one in ten survived the operation, according to the doctor who operated on me. I recovered because my parents and the Sisters all prayed so hard for me. It was then that I began to be aware of the existence of suffering in our lives and of the possibility of bearing it out of love.

Which of your parents had the greatest influence in your upbringing?

I'm not sure. I think both of them were important to me in different ways. I think I got staunch faith and moral integrity from my mother, while dad taught me about standing up for what I believed in. But I learnt a great deal more than that from both of them.

I remember one incident at school that gives some hint of what my life would be like in the future, in that it was to be a life of love for others, a readiness to put myself in the other person's place, to 'live the other' and, at the same time, it gives you an idea of mother's moral severity. I was in middle school, and one day we had a substitute mathematics teacher who didn't know us. I was good at mathematics, and when the teacher began to test us one by one, in alphabetical order starting from 'z', I wasn't at all bothered. But the girl whose turn it was before mine was really scared and told me in sign language that she wasn't going to go up to the board when her name was called out. I whispered back that I would go up instead of her as soon as her name was called, and so I did and solved the problem she'd been set and got a mark of nine. It was only on my way back to my seat that I suddenly realized that my own name was about to be called out. All of a sudden, I panicked but at that very moment the school bell rang and the class was dismissed. I had been saved by the bell.

As soon as I got home, I proudly told mother all about it. She promptly scolded me and said, 'You cannot deceive people like that and you shouldn't lie.'

Were there other important people in your childhood apart from your family, like a teacher, a parish priest, a relation or a friend?

Someone I remember in a very special way is Sister Caroline, one of the Sisters of the Child Mary who was very fond of me. She had a deep love for Our Lady which she passed on to the rest of us. During a visit I made to see her shortly before her death, she said, 'Silvia, remember Mary.' She died like a saint and I have never forgotten her words.

Poverty as a Grace

Silvia grew up, became an adolescent and got to know the world around her. What are your memories of that time?

As I mentioned before, after having been quite comfortable, the family was financially ruined during the general economic crisis. This meant that we were poor, although it was a dignified poverty. I don't regret that period, in fact I see it as a grace, because when at the beginning of the Movement, we started visiting the poor of Trent, I thanked God for having known what it was like to be poor myself. It was an advantage and, compared to my friends, I felt privileged.

It was really mother and dad who felt the poverty most. Whatever they had, they gave to us, and we accepted the situation with a certain amount of humour. It was then, at thirteen years of age while still attending school myself, that I started tutoring other children in mathematics and other subjects, so that I'd have something to contribute at home.

How were you thought of at school? Did you have any special problems, worries or disappointments or did you enjoy school?

I did well at school. I had good friends and we used to help one another. School was an enjoyable experience. The only teacher I disagreed with was a philosophy teacher because, although I found his classes stimulating, I had, thank God, a very strong faith and when this teacher, a non-believer, used to criticize religion, I used to feel sad and annoyed, especially because I thought that my friends might be influenced by him. There wasn't a lesson when I didn't put up my hand in order to express my own beliefs or quite simply to contradict him. I used to say, 'It's not true!'

When he wrote out our assessments, I discovered that he had given me top marks, and some years later, when I happened to meet him again, he confided, 'I've started praying to the God you believe in.'

Did you have some idea then of what your future would hold or were you completely in the dark about it?

Some of my friends and I belonged to the Young Students' Catholic Action. I used to go to meetings where I got to know more about my faith and about practising it. I got quite a lot out of these meetings, but I neither spent time thinking about my future nor had any idea about what my vocation would be, except, perhaps, for some vague inkling.

I remember one day, on the feast of St Thomas Aquinas, I felt such a strong call to holiness that I told a friend of mine and the leaders of Catholic action. Another time it seemed to me that God was asking me whether I was ready to be a martyr.

In my last year at school, something happened that caused me great distress. I had applied for a scholarship to the Catholic University, because I thought I'd have the chance to learn more about God there. They offered thirty free places, and I was the thirty-third on the list and was automatically rejected. I was terribly disappointed and didn't get over it until I felt God saying in my heart: 'I will be your teacher myself.'

You have talked about Love all your life and by it you mean an absolute love but there's another sort of love too, love with a little 'l', earthly love. Have you ever felt this love for someone?

I remember as an adolescent, once seeing a boy to whom I felt attracted, but that's all. My own way was revealed to me quite early on, and I had little time for anything apart from my studies, my involvement with Catholic Action and my passion for spiritual things. These completely filled my life.

Have you never yearned for children of your own?

No, never. Instead, God has given me the incomparable gift of spiritual maternity towards so many people.

You became a primary school teacher and a student of philosophy. What particular memories do you have of those years?

I taught in several places: two little village schools near Trent, and then in an orphanage. I loved my pupils and they loved me. In the afternoons there used to be a rest period when the children would quietly put their heads on their desks and I remember how I used to feel the urge to bless them as a mother would her children and to pray for their futures. I remember also how I used to invent games so as to help them learn things more easily.

In the village of Castello d'Ossana where I had my first teaching post, I set up a branch of Catholic Action. When I was studying philosophy I used to look forward to the oral exams, which gave me the chance to tell the professors who were often non-believers how much truth their notes contained, hoping to motivate them into searching for more.

A New Spirituality

When did you start being called Chiara instead of Silvia?

The orphanage school in Trent where I taught was run by the Capuchin Franciscans. Everything I heard about St Francis and St Clare fascinated me, so when I joined the Third Order of St Francis, I took the name Chiara (Clare) after St Clare of Assisi, because I admired her exclusive choice of God.

It wasn't long, however, before it became clear that the spirituality the Lord had prepared for me and for others would be new and modern and suited to our times. It would stand out clearly from other spiritualities and would help them to be more fully themselves.

Was there any incident which in some way presaged what would happen in the future?

As a child I used to go to the exposition of the Sacrament at the Church of the Blessed Sacrament. I used to gaze at the host, Jesus in the Eucharist exposed in the monstrance, and I'd say, 'You who created the sun which gives light and warmth, through these eyes of mine fill my soul with your light and your warmth.' I said this over and over again, until in the end the host would seem black and the surrounding darkness white.

Separation

*Was it hard to leave your family, your work and your friends
to set out on a venture that would change your life?*

Yes it was, but by God's grace I was able to do it. The
crucial moment was during the war one night when we
had fled our home and were sleeping in some woods
above our house called 'Drop of Gold'. Trent had been
badly hit and our house had been too badly damaged
to stay there: we would have to set out to seek shelter
elsewhere.

The first stirrings of the Movement had already begun, so I felt I ought to stay behind in Trent. Yet how
could I leave my family without even a roof over their
heads? I can't remember how long I cried that night
because of this dilemma, lying out in the open, gazing
up at the stars overhead, but I do remember that at one
point a quotation from Virgil, which I'd read at school,
suddenly came to mind. It was, 'Love conquers all', and
it seemed like an answer from God. 'All, all, all?' I asked
myself. 'Could love resolve even this?' That is when I
said my 'Yes'.

Did your parents understand or did they oppose you?

My father understood right away and gave me both his
permission and his blessing, but my mother was against
it. You see, I was the only one earning money through
the private tuition I gave, and she couldn't understand
why her daughter, who had always been the one to help
the family, had decided at the worst possible moment
to go away and leave them. Later on, though, she gave

me her full support and lived happily close to us until she was ninety-four.

In the 'Little House of Loreto'

What was your first spiritual insight?

I was in Our Lady's shrine at Loreto, where I was staying for a Catholic Students' meeting in 1939. I had no idea what God was planning for me and wasn't even thinking about my future.

The first time I entered the 'little house', which is situated within the fortress-like basilica, I felt deeply moved. It didn't occur to me to wonder whether the legend about it having been the original home of the Holy Family was true or not. I was just alone and completely absorbed in the mystery it represented. In fact, as I meditated on the angel's annunciation to Mary and the life of Jesus, Mary and Joseph together, I found myself crying, which was something I rarely did.

As I touched the stones and wooden supports of those walls and prayed, I imagined how Joseph would have built the house, how the voice of the child Jesus might have echoed there. In my mind's eye, I imagined him crossing the room and thought how blessed were those walls within which Mary would have talked and sung.

While the other girls stayed at the college, I used my free time to return to the 'little house', and each time I had the same experience of feeling deeply moved as if touched by a special grace to the point of being overwhelmed. It was an experience of contemplation and of prayer in the company of those three, Jesus, Mary and Joseph. The Catholic Students' meeting came to an end with a mass celebrated in the basilica which I remember was packed with people that day. I followed the mass with all my heart and, suddenly, I understood that I had found my vocation and that many, many others would follow it too.

The Fourth Way

Was there anyone you shared this with or confided in? Did anyone encourage you and support you?

After that experience at Loreto, I went back to Trent feeling very happy. I knew nothing more than what I've just told you. However, there was a priest who asked me how I'd got on at Loreto, and so I told him that I had discovered my way. 'What is it then', he asked. 'Is it marriage?' 'No', I replied. 'Is it to be a dedicated single woman in the world?' My answer was again 'No'. 'It's the convent then?' he continued. Again my reply was 'No'.

In the 'little house' of Loreto, I had understood in a mysterious way, but with an absolute certainty, that my vocation was to be another way, a fourth way. This fourth way would focus on the Holy Family with virgins and married people together, all equally dedicated, although differently, to God. In other words, it was the Focolare.

I didn't need encouragement or support because everything carried on as before until 1943.

III

Going to the Roots

A Major Lesson

*'While the bombs were falling on Trent, in the air raid shelters
. . .' That's how the story of the Movement starts. Can you
tell me about those days, about the fear, the suffering you saw
around you and how you hoped to overcome all this?*

I have to go back to my family and the night after that
terrible bombing, when we were going back home to see
if anything could be salvaged from the house. It was
then that I told my father and mother that I had decided
to stay on in Trent.

My family was just leaving, setting off along the road
to the mountains. It was a heart-breaking moment, but
I was certain that I was doing the right thing. It was still
very early in the morning, so I turned towards the
bombed city centre. The road was deserted with trees
uprooted all over the place and chaos everywhere. I was
going to see if my friends were alive and, in fact, I found
them all safe.

On my way I met a woman. She seemed to be out of
her mind as she grabbed hold of me screaming, 'Four of
mine are dead!' In comparison to her suffering, my own
seemed so small, and it was there I decided that, from
then onwards, I would care for the suffering of other
people.

43

As the war and its destruction continued, my friends and I tried to give a meaning to our lives. All our youthful dreams fell apart. The girl who had been looking forward to a family of her own received the tragic news of her fiancé's death at the front, the one who had had great hopes for her studies couldn't get to the university because of the road blocks, the one who was planning to set up a beautiful home saw it destroyed by the bombs, and so on. Each of us discovered how frail our dreams had been, but, at the same time, it was as if the war was teaching us an important lesson, that 'all is vanity':[9] everything passes. We couldn't give our all to such transitory things.

We asked ourselves, 'Is there an ideal worth giving our lives to? Is there an ideal that won't fail us and that no bomb can destroy?' The answer was clear. There was such an ideal; it was God.

So together we decided to make God our ideal. Amidst the terrible scenes of war, the result of hatred, God gave us this grace enabling us to understand who he really is: Love.

It's true that before this, we had believed in God and had tried to love him, but it was as if we gained a new understanding of him. This discovery of a truth that had previously escaped us, that God is Love, was like a thunderbolt from heaven for us. It meant that he loved us. It meant that everything that happened, all the joy, all the suffering, everything, was part of his plan, willed or permitted by his love. Our lives took on a new meaning. God showed himself as our Father and we felt we were his children.

This certainty, this belief in his love, affected us so deeply that we agreed that should we too end up as victims of the war, we would want the headstone on our single tomb to be engraved with the words believed in love'.[10]

The New Commandment

Mightn't your 'new' belief in God's love have been the effect of your high emotional state in a time of war? How can you be sure that it wasn't to some extent a form of escapism or evasion of reality?

I think you could've been right if it had remained merely an emotional experience. What happened afterwards gives a better idea of what our 'discovery' really meant.

The first thing we thought of was the words of the Gospel: 'Not everyone who says to me, "Lord, Lord" will enter the kingdom of Heaven, but only those who do the will of my heavenly Father.'[11] So the way we could love God was by doing God's will, and we wanted to do just that from morning till night in the most practical way, even if it should cost us our lives, as when we lingered to help the old and infirm get to the cover of the shelters although the bombing had already started.

Indeed, the shelters to which we fled during the air raids provided scant protection from injury, so we were constantly aware that at any moment we could find ourselves in the presence of God. This made us even more determined to spend what could be the last hours of our lives doing what would be most pleasing to him. It seemed to us that the answer lay in the commandment which Jesus describes with the words: 'my' and 'new'. He says: 'This is my commandment: love one another

45

..s I have loved you. There is no greater love than this, that someone should lay down his own life for his friends'.[12]

Towards Unity

We looked one another in the eyes and promised, 'I am ready to die for you.' 'I for you.' 'All for each.' This was the foundation, you could say, the cornerstone which was to support the whole of the Movement.

But if we were ready to give our lives for one another it was obvious that we had to try to respond to the thousands of demands involved in mutual love. It meant the sharing of our joys, our sufferings, our few possessions, our own spiritual experiences. . . and we threw ourselves into doing this with the whole of our hearts.

Living out the new commandment with this commitment brought changes both within us and around us. There was a clear improvement in the quality of our spiritual lives; we knew a peace, a joy and and a sense of certainty we hadn't experienced before. We discovered a new light within ourselves.

Just as the Fathers of the Church point out, the living of the new commandment made us experience the fullness of Jesus' promise: "Where two or three meet together in my name, I am there among them".[13] So Jesus was spiritually present in our midst, and the joy, the peace and the light we experienced were the fruits of his Spirit.

Moreover, his presence among us was Jesus himself witnessing to the world: 'May they be one. . . that the world may believe. . .' 'If there is this love among you, then everyone will know that you are my disciples'.[14] This is why people were attracted to this new ideal and why so many felt they had to change their lives.

From what you are saying about that early spiritual adventure, it sounds like a group experience of constant happiness, as if difficulties and pitfalls almost didn't exist.

No, not at all. Just the opposite in fact. It wasn't at all easy to live the new commandment the way Jesus meant us to. Keeping his presence among us was quite hard and there were times when we would have felt completely at a loss if we hadn't had the secret, the key to this kind of life.

We understood what the key was when we realized one day that Jesus' greatest suffering in life was when he cried out on the cross: 'My God, my God, why have you forsaken me?' That was when he experienced his inner passion, when burdened by our sins, he felt himself, just like one of us, to be abandoned by the Father. It was then that he broke through the barrier of sin which separates us from God and from one another.

When we understood this, we felt compelled to love him crucified and abandoned, to choose him forsaken and to follow him forsaken.

It is in this love for him forsaken that we have been able and continue to find union with God and communion among ourselves, always rebuilding it and deepening it.

In the Gloom of the Shelters

At one point in your existence you were called the 'Movement for Unity'. Why was that? What happened in your story to give you this characteristic?

There was a specific incident that occurred one day during the war when we were sheltering from an air raid in a gloomy cellar with only the light from a candle. We had the Gospel with us, and the page where we opened it contained Jesus' prayer to the Father before his death: 'May they all be one, as you, Father, are in me, and I am in you, so also may they be in us. . .'[16]

Although the passage wasn't an easy one for us, we felt that not only did we have a certain understanding of it, but that we had been born for it, and that it was the Magna Charta of the Movement which was coming to life. We felt that we had been called to make a contribution to the fulfilment of the unity Jesus spoke about in his testament.

In fact, everything in the Gospel attracted us, so much so that it would be hard to imagine anything other than that little book, the unchanging Gospel, everyone's Gospel, as our rule of life. Gradually, as we tried to put the Gospel teachings into practice, one by one, God began to impress on our hearts those that would become the 'working principles, the motivating ideas',[17] as Paul VI would call them, of a new spirituality in the Church, which would be a specifically collective one. These main ideas were the points of the spirituality I mentioned earlier on: unity and faith in God as love, the will of God, the new commandment, Jesus in the midst of those who are united, the mystery of Jesus forsaken, the Word. . .

Our aim was unity and that is how we came to be called the Movement for Unity.

Isn't the Gospel Enough?

You talk of a 'new spirituality'. What do you mean by spirituality? Some of the terms you use sound complicated compared to simple and basic words like 'Gospel'.

To be honest, I can't think of a word other than the one the Church herself has used for thousands of years. Think of the Franciscan, the Ignatian, the Carmelite spiritualities which are all ways of living the same Gospel but with different approaches. They represent how various great followers of Jesus read the Word of God and put it into practice. These great saints whole-heartedly embraced and practised the founding truths and teachings of the Church according to their particular way of living the Gospel which was the fruit of a charism, a special gift from God.

While our experience is a fairly modest one, we have nevertheless re-meditated and lived out some of the Church's truths and great realities in the light of the charism of unity.

Take the Eucharist for example. Although we never directly urged people to frequent communion, almost everyone started to go to communion often, if not every day. Perhaps it was the presence of Jesus among us which brought an appreciation of Jesus in the Eucharist, and it was the Eucharist, the bond of unity, which subsequently created that strong union characteristic of the Movement in its entirety as well as in its various parts.

Then there was the unity with the hierarchy of the Church. A sentence of the Gospel which touched us deeply right from the beginning and which I've already mentioned earlier was: 'Whoever listens to you listens to me'.[18] This is why we immediately referred all that was taking place in Trent to our bishop, Monsignor Carlo De Ferrari. Our faith in the presence of Jesus in the ecclesiastical hierarchy always maintained the Movement's deep and warm unity with the Church.

Then there was Mary who, as the perfect disciple of Christ, completely clothed in the Word of God, was our constant example of how to live the Gospel. Having been Christ's mother physically, she was also our model in 'begetting Christ', as Paul VI[19] would say, spiritually 'in our midst' in the world.

And finally the Holy Spirit, the God of unity, the leading figure in our story. If our Movement is animated by a charism, as the Church recognizes it to be,[20] we owe it all to him.

The Very First Focolare

Tell me about a typical day in the focolare in Piazza Cappuccini which was the Movement's first nucleus.

My friends used to go to work in the office while I studied at home and then made lunch for everyone. Fairly regularly both our work and study were interrupted by the sirens which would sound day and night. We would then run to the shelters, taking only the Gospel with us. There we used to open the Gospel and read some of it. It was amazing! We had often heard the words read before, but somehow it seemed completely new. It was as if each word was lit up by a light from within and, sentence by sentence, we began to understand how radical Jesus had intended those words of

his to be. No other words, even in spiritual
compare with what we were reading. Th
versal, for everyone and could be put into ᵖ
were eternal, for all ages, and we felt we ha
just as they were, without watering them down.

'Love your neighbour as yourself.'[21] That's what Jesus
said, 'as yourself', so nobody could be loved less than
that, and right there in the shelters there were many
opportunities to put this into practice. It might be just a
word of encouragement to someone or taking someone's children home or some other thing.

'Treat others as you would like them to treat you.'[22]
The bombed city was full of people who had lost their
homes, hungry people, sick, injured and poor. As soon
as the alarms stopped, we would run to look after as
many as we could.

Of course, we needed food, medicine and clothes. . . .

We gave what we had ourselves, but the Gospel says:
'Give, and gifts will be given you.' What we gave re-
turned many times over. 'Ask and you will receive.'[24]
We always found what we needed.

Seeing the promises of the Gospel come true was like
fuel for the new life we had started. There was nothing
to do but to throw ourselves with increasing commitment and enthusiasm into that evangelical adventure.
Many people were impressed by the way we behaved.
They would ask us why were doing it and what the
secret was behind it all, and so we'd tell them that God
was our ideal and that we wanted to do his will by living
the Gospel. Every day new people joined us.

ᴅe Little Houses Increased in Number

You wrote: 'In a few months there were five hundred of us.'
What did you and your friends have that caught on? When
did you have to start organizing things?

I think that what caught on was this new light that the
Holy Spirit was giving us. Today you'd call it the Movement's charism. Not long after we started, the people
who followed the ideal were scattered in one hundred
and fifty eight towns and villages in just in the region
of Trent, and they all wanted to live the Gospel that like
us they had rediscovered.

We never thought about the need to organize things.
We just went ahead. As these first friends of mine
increased in number, it was impossible to stay together
in one house, so we looked for another. It was like that.
But there was already Someone else who was putting
things in order. It was the Holy Spirit who knew well
the work he was to build over the years.

You first appeared officially when you presented the statute
of the Movement to the Bishop of Trent, Monsignor Carlo de
Ferrari. What was that meeting like?

I don't really remember that particular visit to the Archbishop to present him with the Movement's first statute.
We saw the Archbishop many times during that period
to keep him informed of what we were doing and I
remember him saying on one occasion, 'Digitus Dei est
hic', that is 'Here is the finger of God'!

Monsignor De Ferrari was a prudent man who understood us and loved us. He often said jokingly that

when the time came for him to go to heaven and St Peter would ask him what good things he had brought with him, his reply would be, 'The Focolarine and the young girls from Catholic Action.'

Many people went to him to enquire about us, and he would speak to each of them. Sometime in 1956, he decided to write a general statement about us. I'm a little bit reluctant to read it because it's about us, but since we are now spread all over the world, I think you will see how it demonstrates Monsignor Carlo De Ferrari's far-sightedness. Who knows how pleased he must be now in heaven. This is what it said:

To whom it may concern!

What I think about Focolare can be summed up in a few words. I witnessed its birth in my diocese and I have always regarded it as an exceptional company of very fine souls whose lives were edifying in every respect and whose genuine spirit of charity and zealous sense of apostolate are sure proof that in this poor world, 'set as it is on a course to ruin', there are still Christians who are able to scale the most demanding heights of virtue and mine the deepest recesses of goodness. For twelve years now, I have been vigilant and attentive in my observation of them and, during that time, I have never had cause to reprove them. On the contrary, they have always been, in the fullest sense, a source of comfort and joy, a rare experience for me in more than fifty years of pastoral ministry. I have already said this in the past, I have put it in writing on other occasions, and now I repeat it: Would that there were legions of Focolarini!

Signed: *Carlo De Ferrari, Archbishop*

IV

A Base in Rome

At the Heart of Unity

1948 was important because of your move to Rome? What made you decide to do that? What were your fears and misgivings and what hopes did you and your friends have?

We went to Rome because the Movement had spread as far as Rome. The motive for everything we did was unity, unity with God and among people, the unity that is at the heart of Jesus' testament and the fruit of mutual love. Nobody in the Church had started talking about unity yet, at least as far as we knew. It was spoken about certainly, but in quite another sense, by the communists. In Rome there was a Father Leone Veuthey who had written about unity in various booklets.

We wanted to contact him. We had no fears nor misgivings, nor indeed any particular hopes; we were just following the inner voice.

So you got to know him?

Yes, he was a Conventual Franciscan of Swiss origin and a professor of spiritual theology. We were interested in him because of four pamphlets he had written in which he spoke about unity. As a result of our meeting, he kept in close touch with us and became a friend.

You were a group of young girls from Trent with no backing and limited experience. Had you worked out a plan of action to win over the great city of Rome, chaotic as it was in its post war state? Did you ever consider that both you and your plans may have come to grief?

We have never had a plan of that kind. We were very much aware even then that any plan for the future of the Movement depended not on us but on heaven. We concentrated on trying to live what we felt the Lord was teaching us either directly or through daily circumstances. For important decisions, we sought advice from Fr Giovanni Battista Tommasi, the Superior General of the Order of the Stigmata. He was a man of great wisdom and experience, and the Archbishop had entrusted us to him. As to the possibility of failing, we never gave it a thought.

This Ideal of ours now meant so much to us that everything else took second place whether it was our work, our studies, good health, bad health, living in Rome, Trent or Milan. All the Focolarini have still got exactly the same attitude. When they go far away, they don't feel they are going on the missions. They are always at home wherever they go, because they try to be in God.

The Co-Founder and First Married Focolarino

Tell me about your meeting with Igino Giordani[25] whom you refer to as the co-founder of Focolare; but, first of all, here is something he himself wrote about that same meeting.[26]

'One day I was urged to make time for a caller who was described as "an apostle of unity". It was in the September of 1948, and I was displaying the usual courtesy of a Member of Parliament to potential electors, when a group of representatives of the various branches of the Franciscan Order, including a young lady and a young layman, called on me at Montecitorio. The sight of a Conventual Franciscan, a Friar Minor, a Capuchin and a man and woman of the Third Order of St Francis all united and in agreement seemed a miracle of unity in itself to me, and I told them so.

'The young woman began to speak; I was sure I was about to hear sentimental propaganda about some utopian relief organization or other. But then, as soon as she began to speak, I realized this was different. There was something striking about the tone of her voice. I knew that she was sure of what she was saying and that her conviction had to come from a spiritual source. . . .

'What she said put holiness within reach of all; it tore away the fence separating the lay world from the mystical life, and opened to public view the treasures of a castle to which only a few are admitted. She brought God close: God as a father, a brother, a friend available to all.'

This is the meeting as described by Giordani. Can you tell us what it was for you and then what Igino Giordani meant for the Focolare Movement?

I remember it as a simple conversation. I wasn't aware of the effect it was having on Igino Giordani. I began to understand him better, and to see what he had in his heart when I received a letter from him after returning to Trent. He wrote about Jesus' testament, but in such an enlightened way and with such depth, that I felt he was someone God had led on to our path.

For the Movement, he was above all else, an example. Someone once wrote that if the Gospel throughout the world were to disappear, it should be enough to look at how a Christian lived to be able to rewrite it. Giordani was that sort of Christian. When he departed this earth, thousands of people from all over the world attended his funeral. During the mass there was the reading of the beatitudes and anyone who knew him, knew also that each and every one of those beatitudes had been lived by him.

He was a true Christian and a special Christian. God called him to be a co-founder of this new Work in the Church to which he made an irreplaceable contribution during the last thirty two years of his life.

He had always longed to find a way to fulfil the desire that tore at his soul, a way in which he could be consecrated to God while being married. He had long sought it and in 1948 he met the Focolare Movement which at that time was not even five years old.

He was the one who opened up doors of the Focolare to married people. Till then there had been only celibate men and women. Now many followed him drawn by the call to holiness and consecration fulfilling the plan previously only glimpsed, of virgins and married people gathered together in community, inasmuch as their state permits, on the model of the family of Nazareth.

It was he who gave impetus to the birth of the wider

movements within the Focolare such as the New Families Movement, whose couples make their little family cells into living churches, and the New Humanity Movement, which is committed to bringing a genuine Christian spirit into the fields of work, art, medicine, education, politics and so on.

And again, he was the personification of one of the Movement's most important aims in its work for the unification of the Churches.

He was the person who most helped the Movement to root itself solidly in the Church. Before his death he saw the Movement's branches spread to more than one hundred and forty nations throughout the five continents with all the fruits that came from its evangelical spirit which underlines universal brotherhood and sisterhood, mutual respect and love and unity among all, a spirit which demonstrates itself to be appropriate for our times in a world plagued by tension, discrimination, division and war.

Giordani was one of the most precious gifts heaven ever made to the Focolare Movement.

He gave a great part of his life to this new reality in the Church, to this work which is also known as 'Work of Mary'—'of Mary' since it seems to us that here and now, as at other times and in other places, it is especially Mary, the Virgin, the Mother of the Church and Mother of humanity who is going about her work. Giordani had fallen in love with Mary, and it seems to us that she favoured him by making him one of her elect. Among the many achievements of his life, we believe he also reached sainthood.

The First Focolarino Priest

Are there others who had a similar task to Giordani's alongside you in building the Movement?

Yes, there is someone else who since 1949 has made and continues to make an essential contribution in various fields. It's Fr Pasquale Foresi,[27] the first Focolarino priest whose ordination in 1954, opened the way for several other Focolarini who have since been ordained priests.

Thanks to his ability in theology, we now have the Centre for Theological Studies, which provides a theological grounding for the members of the Movement, as well as presenting the Movement in theological terms to others.

Fr Foresi also played a key role in setting up the *Città Nuova*, our publishing house, working with tireless dedication for many years and encouraging and supporting its sister publishing houses abroad. But we also owe many other foundations to him such as the Mariapolis Centres for the training of members of the Movement and, in a special way, the little town of Loppiano, which has become the model for others of its kind in various parts of the world.

He has been more than someone who worked together with me. Like Giordani, I would describe Fr Foresi as a co-founder of the Movement during the various phases of its evolution. He contributed to its becoming fully part of and accepted by the Church; he was its first ecclesiastical assistant and has had an active role in the formulation of its various statutes.

Fr Agostino Favale[28] begins a brief report on the Focolarini with the words: 'Chiara Lubich ... admits to never having nurtured the idea of founding a movement with a spirituality of its own in the Church'. Is this true?

Yes, it is true. When I consecrated myself to God with a vow of chastity in 1943, which is considered the Movement's date of birth, I certainly had no idea of what was going to happen. I was completely caught up by the fact that I had married God. It was something between him and me. In fact, if anyone had mentioned anything about companions, about a Movement etc., it would have completely ruined the enchantment.

Everything came of its own accord later.

A Path of Suffering

Did the Church's hierarchy understand and support you from the beginning or did you meet with indifference and obstacles? Was it a smooth course from the start or was it uphill to begin with?

In the early years, there was both understanding and support so the Movement had an easy life, though, of course, accompanied by all the inevitable trials that go with an evangelical way of life. The second phase was more of an uphill one.

In fact, in the same extract I already quoted from, Fr Agostino Favale continues: 'The Focolare Movement had to tread its path of suffering before it eventually gained approval'. Further on he explains: 'The structure on which the Movement was based and the spirituality which animated it were sufficiently simple as to cast doubts on its possible acceptance and survival. It contained innovative elements that did not fit into the framework of Canon Law besides which, the spontaneous relationship that sprung up among the Focolarini and their sympathizers was open to misinterpretation and misunderstanding on the part of observers. There were certain expressions and attitudes which were considered a bit fanatical'. Can you tell me something about this 'path of suffering'?

This suffering began when for various circumstances, the Movement was put under the scrutiny of the Holy See. After several years John XXIII granted the first papal approval. Prior to that we did pass through a period of suspense, uncertainty and forsakenness.

Several factors came to the fore for us during those years. First of all, a deep love for Jesus crucified and forsaken which always sustained us. We had chosen him and now he was making himself known to us in grand style. It was an opportunity to prove our genuine love for him. And then there was our strong belief in the Church's maternity which must have come to us directly from heaven. Finally, it was a period of extraordinary fruits. The Movement which had already spread to different parts of Europe now began to reach other continents. We saw the beginning of its ecumenical work and its initial penetration of countries behind the Iron Curtain so as to help the Church in Eastern Europe. It was a time of blessings, of immense blessings: 'unless a grain of wheat falls into the earth and dies, it remains alone; but if it dies, it bears much fruit.'[29]

Either Communists or Protestants

What were the most common criticisms of you?

Our emphasis on communion among Christians and, as a consequence, the communion of goods, as well as our efforts to create a dialogue with non-believers drew a lot of suspicion. You know that we put everything in common; this is implicit in our spirituality. You can't say, 'I love my brother as myself', if then you don't share your bread with him. But this choice was, perhaps, too much in advance of the times not to provoke criticism, and there were those who thought we were communists.

Others thought we were Protestants because we were constantly reading the Gospel. Obviously these criticisms came from people who didn't know us very well.

How did you feel about the Holy See's investigation?

We felt peaceful about that because Monsignor Montini, the pro-secretary of State who later became Pope Paul VI reassured us saying: 'Being studied by the Holy See will provide you with both protection and security.' The Church has discernment and quite rightly wants to evaluate every new movement in all its connotations.

I remember that three or four religious from different orders came to see us one after the other. They wanted to get to know us and spent time with us. In the end, they made comments and suggestions to help us draw up our statutes.

Meeting the Movement for a Better World

During those years there was an idea of uniting the Focolare Movement with the the 'Better World Movement' founded by Fr Riccardo Lombardi. What do you remember about him, and why didn't the two movements merge?

I got to know Fr Lombardi during the fifties and there was an immediate relationship of mutual respect. I remember the time he came up to the mountains to see us at our Mariapolis of Fiera di Primiero in the August of '57. I was in bed with my collar-bone in plaster after a car accident, so he spent time with the community and then came to see me, and we shared ideas. He had understood us and was much taken by our ideal. He was a Focolarino at heart. The idea of merging the two movements came about because we could recognize the similarities between our two Works. For example, both movements addressed all the vocations within the Church, his from the bishops to the laity and ours, from the laity to the bishops. We both foresaw a new world, a world renewed by the Gospel, in the ideal of Unity, the *Ut unum sint*, according to Jesus' will.

Then both our superiors, who were, for me the Archbishop of Trent and for Fr Lombardi the General of the Jesuits, Fr Janssens, studied the plan and advised us that the merging of our two movements wouldn't be appropriate. Later on, we understood how right they had been and the value of the grace of office in the Church's hierarchy.

Igino Giordani wrote: 'Do not spoil the benefits of suffering with reactions of anger or the inertia of despair. Overcome suffering with love.'[30] From the way you talk about these events, many of which were accompanied by uncertainty and suffering, it seems that your attitude towards suffering wasn't only one of complete acceptance but that there was also an ability to transform them into joy. Is that so?

Yes, we declared our readiness to suffer when we chose Jesus crucified and forsaken, the utmost suffering as our ideal. It was God who urged us to this, but it also had something to do with that youthful generosity which doesn't even fear death. We tried to be true to this. We experienced suffering in the deepest part of our beings, but we tried to embrace the cross and not drag it along with us. It's as if through some divine alchemy, you pass from suffering, to love, to joy.

There has been sorrow and suffering throughout more or less the whole of our history with illnesses, deaths, spiritual trials, also dark nights, absurd situations and so on. These situations have accompanied us and will continue to be present because the cross is the hallmark of a Work of God.

On the other hand, the joy and the consolations God has given us have been so great, so special, so deep and intimate that the world couldn't even begin to imagine them. When God is working in your midst, you experience the mountain peaks and the abysses.

And so you were meeting famous people and asking for meetings with ecclesiastical authorities and political figures without any shyness or embarrassment. What was it that made you so sure of yourselves?

We never felt afraid or uneasy. Every time I met Igino Giordani, he used to give me one of his books, and I would regularly make a present of it to someone else. He used to be amazed, because people generally thought very highly of his books and regarded them as valuable. But for our part, we never saw Giordani in the light of fame and political importance, but rather as a brother, albeit a rather special one.

There was one of our songs, quite an ingenuous song really, which used to amuse De Gasperi, so much so that he wanted us to sing it for him when he came to our summer Mariapolis at Fiera di Primiero. It went like this: 'Bus drivers and students, doctors and chemists and Members of Parliament—all gathered here in the Mariapolis already are equal. What do the jobs matter if here we are brothers?'

De Gasperi, a Focolarino?

De Gasperi was one of us in the same way as those we call adherents belong to the Movement. They are people who take the Ideal to heart in a real way. I met him for the first time in Fregene with Giordani and a group of young people from the Movement. We met on other occasions and we corresponded. In a letter of 21 April 1951, he wrote to me:

'. . .Feeling united beneath the wings of divine paternity brings a sense of serenity and trustfulness even in the hour of tribulation. These are troubled times in which those who are responsible for governing are gripped by doubt. Our country faces bitter days, and we do not have the necessary solidarity and unity to meet the tragedy ahead. If I were not obliged to share in the responsibility for that piece of history which Providence has given over to the free will of humanity, I should

65

have withdrawn and resigned myself to God's will. But for the Christian who understands politics as the outward expression of his faith and, above all, as a means of working for the social community and therefore supremely answerable to the community and to the common Father of us all, that anguish-fraught labour becomes an inescapable duty'.

In another letter of 28 December 1953, De Gasperi wrote:

'As usual during these days, I don't have the peace I would like to be able to dedicate time to my best friends. There are fresh troubles, new difficulties to resolve'. He asked me to pray to the Lord: 'Not for me, but for our troubled country. . .'

A Living Christian Community

You are fond of speaking of 'rediscovering' the Gospel. Aren't two thousand years enough to have exhausted the Gospel's content? What's new in Chiara Lubich's rediscovery?

I'm convinced that neither two thousand, nor three thousand, nor any amount of time is sufficient to extract from the Gospel all the wealth it contains, because of the simple fact that it is God's Word and therefore inexhaustible. But he is the one who has got to explain it, interpret it and make us discover it as new and fascinating.

This happened for us, as I explained, in the air-raid shelters when we used to take the Gospel with us. At those times, it seemed to us to be the only book worth reading and preserving in the event of total destruction.

I must admit that until then I hadn't seen the Gospel as a formula for living, but when my friends and I started to live it, both our relationships with God and with other people started to change. To understand this better, you must remember that up till then, we had at the most tried to meditate on the Word, to penetrate it with our minds and extract some considerations or resolutions from it.

But now something very different was happening. The Word was being taken on board with all its consequences in the context of our daily lives, and it had a transforming effect at both an individual and a group level. When the Word was lived, it was no longer a matter of living, so to speak, as me or us, but the Word present in me, the Word present in the group, and the result of this was the Christian revolution with all its consequences.

Those who looked on from outside were astounded, I remember, to find that instead of a meditation on the Gospel, they were looking at a living Christian community. Some of them imagined that we must have been involved in some quite outlandish form of meditation on the Word of God.

God didn't ask us to prioritize the building of hospitals, orphanages, schools or other good works. We do have these, but they came later. God drew our attention to the Gospel; he let us see it in a new light and gave us a way of understanding it that was suited to these times. The life of the Word became the cornerstone and the driving force for an ongoing formation at every stage of our spiritual lives.

Mary: The First Lay Person

You understood the importance of the laity in the Church long before the Second Ecumenical Council, didn't you?

When my companions and I set out on our experience of rediscovering the Gospel, we weren't thinking about the question of the laity in the Church. We were profoundly aware of our calling to live the Gospel. We didn't think of ourselves as lay people so much as Christians. Jesus' prayer for the *Ut unum sint*, his promise to be present among two or three united in his name, the invitation to follow him taking up our crosses and all his other words seemed to be addressing us in an all-embracing way, although we were neither nuns nor priests, and they made us feel ourselves to be wholly Church.

At that time we were all lay people and even now the majority of us are lay, and this is why Mary has great importance in our Movement. We always saw and see in her the 'first lay person'. We see her as virgin and spouse, housewife and seat of wisdom and while remaining in the background, involved in the work of evangelization as she follows her Son in public life, at Cana, beneath the cross and supporting the apostles in the newly born Church.

We also see her involved at a social level with the Magnificat which we consider to be the Magna Charta of the Christian social message. Mary can be seen as the obvious model for the laity with its tasks and responsibilities in the Church and in the world.

Why does our age need committed lay people more than other periods in history?

One of the reasons, I think, may be that sometimes people today are so caught up in scientific and technological progress and so swept along by the frenetic pace of life that they have neither time nor inclination to listen to words about a God they no longer feel they really need. This is why it has been said: 'Today we need witnesses more than teachers.'[31] This doesn't mean that there is no need to proclaim the Gospel through words, but it will be received better if it is witnessed in every day life, outside the churches, in the secular world, on the streets, in the factories, in the schools, in the offices, in scientific laboratories and in parliaments.

Only those who mingle with the men and women of our times, sharing their day to day existence, are able to give this witness. It's only, or rather more often, the lay person who can do this. It's possible, above all, for Christians committed to living in such a way that Christ is present in today's world, so that he can continue to redeem and free people. He has to be born and come alive again not only in the eucharist but also in the human heart and among people. This is why, right from the beginning and before everything else, the important thing for us has been to fulfil his promise: 'Where two or three are gathered in my name, there I am in the midst of them.'

The Call

Are those who follow the Movement responding to a call, or are they searching for a meaning to their lives, or perhaps escaping from some painful situation, or attempting to overcome some personal dissatisfaction, or what other motive do they have?

Those who follow the Movement are undoubtedly re-sponding to a call. It's almost always the case that whenever the Movement is presented or its spirit is explained, there are those who understand it, who grasp its beauty and the uniqueness of this charism and feel drawn to make it their own, and then there are those who don't understand. Those who understand it are the ones God calls. They are not always the good ones, the better ones, but the ones that he chooses.

But before that happens, of course you can't deny that people will have the widest possible conditions within them, which can urge them to escape an unsatisfying life, or to wish for new relationships, or to need a genuine family and so on. This may be part and parcel of their search and may later play its part in confirming their incentive to adhere to what they have found. But in the Movement itself, we are talking about a genuine call from God.

V

The Focolare Spirit

How did it get its name?

*You get to know the Focolare Movement starting with its
name or rather with its various names: The Focolare Movement, The Work of Mary, The Movement for Unity. Why are
there so many of them? Shouldn't you choose one to avoid
confusion apart from anything else?*

The Movement's history spans half a century and it
acquired these various names during the different
stages of its development. We didn't choose the first
name, Focolare.[32] Someone just started calling the little
groups of men or women, focolares. The name stuck
and it suited us. I spoke earlier of how we wanted to
emulate in some way the family of Nazareth which was
composed of virgins who among them had Jesus, the
flame of the hearth.

We were also called the 'Movement for Unity' because of our new concept; but we finally ended up with
the name: 'Work of Mary' which I think describes our
spirituality best of all, even though we still call ourselves, and have others call us, Focolarini.

'You Are a People'

How is the Movement organized?

Before I talk about the Movement's structure and its branches and so on, I'd like to say that, first of all, we see ourselves and all who belong to the Movement as a single body, just one entity. The unity we speak about is something which has to be true for us and lived out among us before everything else. It's only on this basis that we can then communicate the message of unity to the world. This is really the only way to explain the identity of the Movement. We see and feel ourselves as one. Pope John Paul II sees us in this light too and, perhaps on account of the numbers of people in the Movement, he has addressed us with words such as these: 'You are a people', which I think is an apt description of the Movement, which is a people or a portion of the Church.

The differences are secondary. They consist of various vocations with various tasks, but always with the same end in sight.

During the forty-seven years of its existence, the Movement has spread to one hundred and fifty six nations with the result that there are now millions of people whose lives are influenced in one way or another by the spirituality of unity. Of these, eighty thousand are adults who are either consecrated with vows or promises or who have made another sort of serious commitment to the Movement.

The nature of the Movement and its spirit as well as its aims and infrastructure are defined in a statute which was revised and approved by the Holy See on 29 June 1990. In addition to the general statute for the whole of the Movement, there are also internal rules of life for the twenty-two different branches that make it up.

The Movement throughout the world is divided into sixty-six geographical zones. The International Centre, the nerve centre, if you like, for the whole of the Movement throughout the world, is at Rocca di Papa, near Rome. This centre assures the unity and co-ordination of the Movement's various branches and activities.

The pivotal supports of the Movement are the several new vocations that have blossomed within it. The first to emerge were the men and women Focolarini. They live as groups either of men or of women, in the focolare houses and are immersed in the world and go out to work like everyone else. They have left behind, however, their countries, their families, in fact everything. These focolares are a new type of little community, whose members try to keep the presence of Jesus among them by living mutual love in all they do. The evangelical counsels of poverty, chastity and obedience are seen as supports to maintain this unity by being detached from possessions, from other people and from oneself.

For the Movement as a whole, the focolares are like burning points of light. They are the guardians of that flame which is our love for God and for our neighbour: a flame that must never die.

The innovative element of these communities of evangelical life is the fact that they include married people who belong in a complete way and not as second class members. These married members have also been called to give themselves completely to God while fulfilling all the commitments of their married state. There are almost five thousand men and women Focolarini.

These focolares are at the heart of a Movement that calls itself lay and yet, if you excluded the married members, they would resemble, an almost monastic way of life. Would you agree?

It's true that if there were only the focolares, that might appear to be the case. But right from the start, the Movement was much wider than the focolares and always had a definite lay identity—apart from which, the term lay is completely suitable for the Focolarini themselves.

In any case, from 1956 onwards, the Movement's lay nature was revealed even more clearly with the dramatic emergence of the vocation of the men and women Volunteers. These are lay people who want to answer the call to holiness like the Focolarini and who bind themselves to the Movement with special 'commitments'. They strive in living out the Gospel to bring new life and renewal to their social environment through their witness at a professional, family and political level. They too spend some essential time in the community life of their 'nuclei'. At present there are more than seventeen thousand Volunteers.

To continue on the 'lay' theme, a large section, and perhaps the most important one for the future of the whole Movement, is the new generation: the Gen, made up of girls and boys, including young adults, youth and children over the whole age range. These young people take up the spirituality of the Movement and make it their own, living it with great generosity, or I should say, living it with all their hearts according to their own specific guidelines. They also meet up in little groups, called Gen units, which provide them with a meeting point and the means to prepare themselves to take this spirituality out to other young people in the schools, the universities, to their sports and leisure clubs and to their musical and artistic activities etc.

So far it's quite clear. The Focolarini, the Volunteers and the Gen are the most committed members, but although they account for several thousands I still don't have the complete picture of the scope and diversity of the Movement which encompasses several million people who share in your way of life in one way or another.

In the last two decades or so, there have been further developments. Since every member and every section of the Movement has an outreach through their lives, there has been what you might call a spontaneous ripple reaction around these more committed members, with vast numbers of people being attracted to the Movement through the witness they have seen. For example, around the married Focolarini there is now the 'New Families Movement', around the men and women Volunteers has developed the 'New Humanity Movement' and the life of the Gen has brought about the movements: 'Young People for a United World' and 'Youth for Unity', the first for young adults and the second for younger teenagers and children.

Beneath the Mantle

Yes, all this is 'lay' and for lay people, and yet it's a fact that there are priests, men and women religious in the Movement.

To explain this, I'd like to draw a parallel. Many people, I think, have seen and admired the sort of frescoes in medieval churches which depict a devotion to Mary which was popular in those times. I'm thinking now of the one that shows the Virgin Mary wearing a great mantle which enfolds and protects castles and churches, craftsmen and monks, bishops and mothers of children, the rich and the poor—all the people that made up a city of those times. More than being an excessive expression of devotion, it was more a way of depicting the relationship which the Mother of God has with the Church, with humanity. It's a way of representing her universal motherhood which is one of the cardinal points of our faith.

It's much the same with us. Instead of a great fresco, the Movement is a bit like a living copy of that image, of what the image represents. In a way that resembles Mary, this Work of hers is like a mantle that gathers together whole sections of the Church and humanity, because God has given it the gift of creating a family out of them. It's a gift, a charism that makes the Movement resemble Mary in her maternal and unifying role.

In fact, there are both seminarians, or 'Gen's' as we call them, and diocesan priests, and around them has come to life the Parish Movement. Right from the beginning, the spirit of the Movement spread among the members of many religious families, both men's and women's, bringing great spiritual benefits to them.

For several years now there have also been bishops, friends of the Movement, from all over the world who meet up together from time to time. The spirituality of unity helps them to focus in a particular way on real and loving collegiality with the Holy Father, among themselves and with their brother bishops. There are about seven hundred of them to date and their activity has always been encouraged, first, by Paul VI and now by John Paul II.

What are the characteristics of the priests and religious who are members of the Movement?

If the Movement is like a rough sketch of the Church, it can't be without priests, monks and nuns. They have been present since the beginning. One might ask what attracted them then, and what still attracts them today? Both then and now, the motives are the same. They were often virtuous, humble, patient and saintly people, but in the Movement they have discovered, in a new way, that as well as preaching the Gospel, they have first of all to live it. Many priests have found once again the flavour and freshness of the Gospel, and the transforming effect of this can be seen in both their private lives and their ministries.

They too have discovered, like the lay people, that Christianity isn't only an individual relationship with God, but communion with God and with your neighbour, and hence the possibility of living with others in the way of the Trinity, in the image and likeness of God. It follows that the priest is no longer isolated and inaccessible.

But it is the entire spirituality that has changed their outlook. The rediscovery of God who is Love, the choice of him as the ideal of their lives, enables them to stop seeing their ministerial priesthood as an absolute, since the only essential value is God and, although their ministerial priesthood is an extraordinary vocation, it is nothing other than the mission to which they have been called, to carry out his will as true servants of humanity.

They have found their identity and their ideal in Jesus crucified, the priest and victim. They themselves say that this dimension enriches their pastoral activity and, for our part, we have seen that they become free of the sort of clericalism which people today dislike so much.

On the other hand, they live in such close contact and communion with the whole family of the Work of Mary, in which the unity of all in the royal priesthood precedes any regard for roles, that they cannot be misled by the status of a role, because Mary constantly reminds them that what matters is love and God and, if their ministry isn't one of love and service, their priesthood is in conflict with that of Christ.

Neither Assistants nor Chaplains

Why do you train your own priests instead of having someone from the vast vineyard of God serve as assistant or chaplain to your lay movement?

The diocesan priests I have spoken about so far, live the spirituality of the Movement but are, obviously, under the jurisdiction of their own bishops and dioceses. The most committed of them number about one thousand four hundred around the world, and there are twelve thousand adherents or sympathizers.

But in addition to these, there are others who entered the focolares as lay people and who were later called to the priesthood. As the Movement expanded throughout the world, we felt the need to have our own priests whose long experience of life in focolare in addition to their professional life in society would be more suited to the needs of a lay movement. So after the requisite preparation, some of these Focolarini who had worked as doctors, workers, engineers, teachers and architects, were ordained 'to be at the service of the Work of Mary'. Their model is Mary, who is not a priest but the Mother of the supreme and one Priest, in whom alone do priests have meaning. She is the incarnation of that Gospel which, since its essence is charity, will remain in the next life, where there will be no hierarchy nor sacraments.

We don't call them either assistants or chaplains. Before everything else they are Focolarini, although, because of the grace of their ministry and their particular training, they can perform a valuable priestly service throughout the whole of the Movement and at its centre.

A Religious Twice Over

How do you explain the presence of so many monks and nuns in the Movement which is so clearly a lay one? Don't they already have a their own way to holiness well marked out for them in their own rules and spiritualities?

I'd like to reply to this question by reading something from Fr Castellano Cervera[33]. It's from the introduction to my book *Unity and Jesus Forsaken*,[34] the two sides of a medal that sums up our spirituality. He writes:

'In their complete interdependence, unity and Jesus forsaken constitute an absolute innovation in Christian spirituality. They are a revelation, a charism, a gift for the Church today, open as it is to the mystery of unity and so much in need of discovering, in a world like our own, the face and the heart of Jesus forsaken present in humanity. . . .

'Unity and Jesus forsaken, the peaks of Jesus' experience, are not simple aspects of Christian spirituality alongside others but the summits of the Gospel from which the originality of Christ's message shines forth.

'These two things, unity and Jesus forsaken, represent both the summit and summary of Christian spirituality. They do not only contain in themselves the classic elements of Gospel spirituality, but they shed light on them and combine them in the harmony of God's plan.

'They are universal principles which can be lived by everyone, of all vocations, both individually and collectively. They enable us to live according to the Spirit of Jesus and to share in his feelings of love, in unity and the inseparable experience of death and resurrection, in the continuous and luminous passage from suffering to love, and to live all of this with the same Spirit as the Crucified-Risen Lord.'

These authoritative words contain the reason why numerous men and women religious belong to the Movement. They are helped by our spirituality and its 'universal principles which can be lived by everyone', and they find that it illuminates their own spiritualities 'combining them in the harmony of God's plan.'

Contact with this charism helps religious to understand their own founders better. They see their superiors and their communities with new eyes and contribute to a deeper communion among the members of their communities, whose subsequent renewal often leads to greater numbers of vocations. A new awareness of their unity with other religious orders, with priests and with the laity often leads them to do more to make the Church a single communion. The men in religious communities who belong to the Movement are now more than nineteen thousand and the women more than forty-two thousand.

The Little Towns

In spite of all you've said, what I still can't understand is how all these different people, the Movements and the branches, manage to feel they are all part of the same family and especially how they manage to keep and strengthen the links among them. Don't tell me that it's enough to have a water-tight structure or to share the same ideals in order to ensure stability and growth in an organization like this.

No, it's only possible when there is an ongoing and thorough formation together with a spiritual imput from the start to the end of one's life. Over the years various means have emerged in the Movement to make it possible, and they have become permanent and indispensable structures.

There are what we call the Mariapolis Centres. Apart from the one at Castelgandolfo which John Paul II gave us, there are thirty-nine others in the different zones. They run formation courses in the spirituality and provide updating on the life of the Movement, but most of all they develop a communion of life, a practice that goes back to the Movement's early days.

Another typical foundation of ours is the series of little towns of witness. At present there are thirteen of them throughout the world, but there are going to be more. They accommodate people from all the different vocations in the Movement, who attend courses of formation related to their specific vocation, and they also offer a witness to our spirituality lived out in work, personal relationships, study and prayer.

At the moment we have little towns in Italy, Africa, Argentina, Mexico, the United States, the Philippines, Spain, Switzerland, one in Germany which has the characteristic of being ecumenical, and two in Brazil. More recently, one has been set up in Melbourne, Australia and another in Belgium. Soon there will be one in Portugal and another in Poland.

Are these little towns all organized in the same way?

They're all different from one another in that they reflect the environment they're in, whichever continent it might be. The first one at Loppiano, near Florence in Italy, has mainly young people, but there are also some families, some priests and religious. There are scores of nations represented, all linked by the commandment of Jesus: 'Love one another as I have loved you'. To the thousands of people who visit it, this little town is a witness of what the world could be like if the Gospel were the law of human society.

The little town in Argentina, O'Higgins, near Buenos Aires is based on agriculture and farming. It teaches land cultivation in a region of extreme social problems.

The little town close to Recife in the north east of Brazil focuses on skills and crafts. It developed in response to the need to give the people who live in the Mocambos slums a sense of human and Christian dignity. They have house-building projects to provide decent homes, schooling and efforts to secure basic jobs.

Another little town, Aracoeli, is near to San Paolo and is mainly a training school for all the vocations in the Movement.

The one at Fontem in Cameroon was built up from next to nothing in the bush. There, whites and blacks have worked together in the building of relief operations such as a hospital, a school, palm oil and brick-making industries. It illustrates, in keeping with Vatican

II, how all the Church should be missionary, and it was begun by lay people who were later joined by priests of the Movement.

The little town of Tagaytay, near Manila in the Philippines, was established in order to become better acquainted with the other world religions and to discover the seeds of the Word contained in the religious traditions of the East, and so focus together on what we have in common. At the same time, we are involved with our Buddhist friends at a social level in projects to help the poor around the outskirts of Manila.

In Switzerland, the little town of Montet, which is more like an international school, is dedicated to training Focolarini and Focolarine (men and women) for life in the focolares. The witness this little town offers and, even more so that of the ecumenical town of Ottmaring in Germany, is a source of great interest to both its Catholic and non-Catholic visitors.

How Difficult is it to Join and Leave?

How do you join the Movement? Are there formal obligations? Are there reasons, and what might be those reasons, for someone to be refused? Is it easy to leave the Movement and does that happen often or seldom and why?

Given the structure of the Movement, belonging to one or other of its branches is representative of a whole range of callings within the framework of the overall vocation of the Movement and the living of its spirit and general aims. There are therefore different commitments depending on whether you belong to the Focolarini, the Gen, the Volunteers or the priests etc.

As to the members of the Movement in a much wider sense, such as the one and a half million adherents, who are involved personally, and who are attracted by the spirituality and take part in a variety of activities, there is complete freedom in their belonging to the Movement, as indeed in their possible withdrawal from it. There are no obligations other than a moral one to follow a way of life that offers food for spiritual growth.

In time, many of these people express the desire to deepen and share with others the spiritual experience they have begun, and they find new and more committed ways to serve the Movement in its various branches.

The Focolarini, the Volunteers and the Gen etc., have a definite responsibility to be faithful to their commitment and are answerable not so much to an organization as to God himself and their own consciences.

One or other branch wouldn't accept those who are not suited to them.

Since the Movement is immersed in the world, it does happen that some people leave for purely worldly reasons, but we have noticed that, after shorter or longer periods of difficulty, they usually return. Their experience of God through the Movement was so strong that they say they were never able to forget it.

No Publicity

Do you do any promotional or advertising activities to gain new members?

From the very beginning, any sort of publicity seemed quite foreign to the nature of the Movement. It was clear to us from the start that new vocations would appear only in as much as we looked for the Kingdom, in which Christ would be present among us. He's the one who calls people.

We are still convinced of this. Nevertheless, despite our outstanding growth in numbers over the years, we always feel how inadequate we are compared to the enormous and serious needs that exist which would require far more workers for the Father's harvest.[35]

We feel that the prayer Jesus suggested in asking for new builders for the Work of God is as necessary now as ever, so we cannot say that those responsible for the Movement don't hope that many might be called. Attention is given to how to increase our numbers.

But our characteristic way of proposing a lifestyle along the lines of the Movement is still that of the early times.

But you publish books and magazines and you use the means of communication and the most advanced technology . . .

In the early days we even felt a bit suspicious of the printed word. We didn't think it was possible for the written word to express a 'divine adventure', a spirit that had to be lived. We felt there was no way of grasping it and making it your own, other than through a personal commitment in communion with other people who were also living it.

Then, during one of our summer gatherings in 1956, as many as a hundred participants made the repeated request to be kept in touch with what would happen after their departure, and so be able to continue sharing in the joys and sufferings of the whole community. This meant a little newsletter had to be written, consisting of experiences and spiritual thoughts that then had to be duplicated, and we used an ancient duplicating machine that worked with pure alcohol.

That was our very first experience of the printed word. We saw it as a new way of practising mutual love.

Then our magazine *New City* came along and our first book: *Meditations*.[36] Now the Movement has eighteen publishing houses. The most advanced of these is *Città Nuova* for the Italian language, but there are publishing houses for other languages: German, French, Spanish, English, Dutch, Portuguese and so on in the different countries.

Apart from this, we now do quite a lot of audio and video recording, so as to have material for the constant updating on the life of the whole Movement and so as to be able to maintain communion among us all. This work has its technical base at Centro Santa Chiara, where two departments specialize in sound recordings and audio-visuals.

An important aspect of this work is the telephonic conference call, when fifty-seven of our centres around the world are simultaneously linked up. It provides us with the means of communicating a 'spiritual thought' and the most important 'news' of the Movement from the centre and the different zones. This monthly rendez-vous is an occasion for the whole Movement to be in communion, and it allows all the members of the Movement to come together and share in each other's joys and sufferings, enabling them to be, wherever they are in the world, one heart and one soul.[37]

What are the most important appointments of the year for the Focolarini?

The annual appointment for all the members in the different zones, for adults and young people, is the Movement's Day Meeting or Mini-Mariapolis.

Everybody looks forward to it, because no matter which branch of the Movement you belong to, this gathering makes everybody aware of the fact that they are one family. It usually focuses on a particular point of the spirituality of unity, an updating on the Movement's life and its members around the world, and a report on the expansion of this ideal of life in new spheres and regions during the past year. The most relevant experiences are also shared.

In addition, it's an opportunity to present the Movement to people who would like to get to know about it. Often relatives and friends who aren't churchgoers come along.

The Summer Mariapolis

Another regular event in the Movement's calendar is the Mariapolis, a summer gathering of several days organized in each zone. It's a practice that started as far back as 1949. The citizens of this temporary city of Mary make every effort to love one another and to live the Gospel, thereby creating as it were, the model for a new society. Like the Day Meetings, the Mariapolises are attended by people from different walks of life and of different age groups and there are priests, lay people and religious. Special attention is given to those for whom God is something remote and to those who are new to the Movement, so that they can get to know it through a living experience.

The wider Movements within the Work of Mary all have their own big events from time to time at the centre of Movement. They last for one or two days and are attended by representatives from all the continents.

What is the purpose of these meetings?

To work together to build a more united world and, with this aim in mind, to find ways of responding to the problems of society, of the family and of youth etc.

The meetings organized by the New Humanity Movement for example explore the ideals of the Gospel in the context of the social reality. There are key talks addressing the most pressing social questions in the light of unity with suggestions and guidelines for action and feedback on projects and activities taking place in different parts of the world and in different cultural spheres. These gatherings are a witness to unity between classes and between groups that are different from one another in every possible way, because participants come together according to their specific area of involvement, such as the world of art, of politics, of education etc. In the congress for the world of health, for example, there would be doctors, nurses, patients, people employed in a whole range of ancillary services. They meet together and compare their experiences so that in unity, they can learn together how to go about building up their small society in Christ.

The meetings of the New Families Movement deal with topics concerning the world of the family such as marital relations, parenting and children, engagement, adoption, separation etc. They are a witness as to how families can be renewed and can acquire an openness to others when unity is lived within the ambit of the family.

The Genfest is the five-yearly festival of the 'Young People for a United World' Movement, at which they assess the work undertaken by the youth all over the world and propose their future plan of action for their various 'ways to unity'. They focus on unity between different generations, people of different ethnic origins, different races and nations, different cultures, different social groupings, between human life and nature and so on. The festival is also a valuable opportunity to influence public opinion and to communicate their message to other young people, but, above all, it's an opportunity to deepen the spirit of unity which they wish to motivate all their activities. The festival programme features action reports, telling about individual and group experiences, drama and mime, dance and music, all of which converges, however, on the overall theme of contributing to the building of a more united world. The 'Youth for Unity' Movement, which works along the same lines as 'Young People for a United World' but with a younger age group, also has its own major events.

The Parish Movement's congresses are aimed at working to make the parish a living community by spreading the spirituality of unity. In this way they consolidate the unity of the faithful around the parish priest, creating a sense of communion among everybody and encouraging co-operation between the different parish organizations.

Openness Towards Others

Other important meetings are organized by the different branches for their own members such as the men or the women who live in the focolares, the men or women Volunteers, the Gen, the priests, the men or women religious.

A feature common to all our gatherings is the participation of people from a wide variety of Churches or Christian denominations, people of other religions, as well as people who don't profess any religion but who are attracted by the spirit of unity characteristic of this family.

We also hold interesting ecumenical conferences at the Centre of the Movement or in those zones which have a particular commitment to Christian unity.

What are the financial resources of the Focolare?

There are three: God's providence, the communion of goods and work.

The members of the Movement trust above all in God's providence. The Gospel's 'Seek first for the kingdom of God and his righteousness, and all the rest will be yours as well'[38] is of fundamental importance for us. If we live the Gospel, we can be sure that God will look after our needs. This is our continuous experience and we are full of gratitude for it. Not only has there always been providence, but it has been abundant, and we see it as the Work of Mary's primary resource.

Then there is the communion of goods. The first community which grew up around Trent during the war consisted of several hundred people, of whom about thirty had serious financial difficulties. All the others committed themselves to giving what they could, month by month, as well as looking for jobs for those who were unemployed. This is how a spontaneous communion of goods came about motivated by love for others. This communion of goods and needs has become a way of life in the economic outlook of the Focolare Movement. Everybody practises it, inspired by the example of the early Christian communities of whom it is written: 'Those who came to faith were of one heart and one soul and all things were in common among them'.[39]

Goods in Common

Each branch of the Movement has its own particular way of carrying out the communion of goods. The Volunteers for example make a commitment to contribute their surplus regularly. They do this in complete freedom and in the light of their family obligations and social responsibilities.

The Gen with their typical enthusiasm and generosity always put everything in common, be it material possessions or talents. Their sense of charity makes them respond immediately to every urgent need both within the Movement and in the world outside, and they involve other young people in their efforts to aid the victims of war and natural catastrophes. The younger ones and even the smallest children are involved in this communion. They may choose to go without favourite toys or take part in any number of activities to find the means of helping other children in need. Quite often they draw adults into their fund-raising ventures.

The priests put their private means into common. They try to respond to the needs of priests in poorer circumstances than themselves, and they share in the communion of goods of the whole Movement.

The communion of goods in the New Families Movement is quite extraordinary. They see the family budget as something that should be lived in the spirit of the Gospel. The communion of goods among them extends to families in other zones and other nations and is inspired by the concept of the universal family. Just recently they have been assisting Lebanese families who were obliged to flee their country. Accommodation, funding and jobs were found in various European countries, and they raised money which continues to support both the families who have remained in Europe and those who have returned to the Lebanon.

And finally the Focolarini. They are called to live Jesus' words on this subject to the letter: 'Whoever of you does not renounce all that he has cannot be my disciple'.[40] Before they finally and permanently enter focolare, they give all that they have and dispose of everything that might come to them on the future. Then, every month, they put all their earnings into common. The married Focolarini also live personal poverty and spiritual detachment in all things. They share in the focolare house's communion of goods with whatever they might have of their own and receive from it for their needs.

Taking account of all this, it would seem that the Holy Spirit has given us a new concept of economics. We are no longer prey to excessive anxiety about saving up and putting things by for the future. There are two new factors in what we do. First of all, it must be said that providence provides in a way we hadn't come across before and that we can now depend on when we draw up our budgets and, secondly, the communion of goods makes us feel the freedom of the poor, a freedom you experience when you give joyfully.

Everybody's a Worker

Our third financial resource is our work. We place great value on the idea of work, as we see it as a means of doing God's will and a way of serving Jesus in the community.

Everybody in the Movement works, including the Focolarini who are called to give themselves completely to God and to the apostolate. We work because Jesus worked. We work because the three members of the household of Nazareth, our original inspiration, were workers. We work, however, with the detachment the Gospel teaches, so we are ready to change jobs or to give up working if we are asked to spend our time working for the development of the Movement. We have seen that everywhere, and especially in Eastern European countries, work done with this attitude and accompanied by the communion of goods among all, becomes an impressive witness to Christianity and, thereby, a door to faith.

Is there any monitoring, any assessment of the administration of goods or an examination of the accounts? What's your criterion for managing these?

As I said before, the spirituality of the Work of Mary is based on the unity that shapes every aspect of our lives including something as practical as our financial management. We want every area of our lives to be the fruit of mutual love.

So it's to be expected that when this principle is applied to our administrative activities, the result should be a gift, a service for others. The administrative dealings in every branch of the Movement reflect the continuous communion among those who are concerned with it, and everything is done with complete openness.

Every branch and every substantial foundation established by the Movement submits regular administrative accounts to our Centre as well as an annual financial report, together with balance sheets and a budget forecast for the forthcoming year. The general rule is that, as far as it is possible, all the branches and institutions should try to be economically self-sufficient.

The life at the Centre of the Movement is supported financially through the communion of goods among the various branches and foundations, while the providence we receive is used for the Movement's apostolate and its development.

The different zones we have throughout the world also give a monthly report on their financial situation and an annual balance of accounts for their various activities.

The Centre of the Movement keeps itself informed of all of this in detail, but it has never been seen as a form of monitoring, rather as an expression of mutual help which gives security.

Since the Movement exists within the framework of society, it adopts the customary legal practices approved by a country's legal system and is subject to the usual laws and fiscal duties laid down by that particular country.

Are you planning to create a more solid legal and economic identity for the Movement or are you satisfied with it as it is?

We have recently had the joy of receiving the Holy See's approval of our revised general statutes which along with the individual rules for each branch reflect the life of the Movement today.

They were approved on 29 June 1990 by the Pontifical Council for the Laity and were officially handed over to us by its president, Cardinal Pironio. These statutes, like the separate rules for the branches, outline our legal and economic identity, and we are satisfied with them.

At the same time, however, we feel we have to be open to further developments, whatever they might be, should the Holy Spirit indicate them, should he want them.

VI

Dialogue

Good Neighbours

Are you on good terms with other big movements such as Catholic Action, Communion and Liberation, the Scouts?

Our aim, as I've said, is to work in and with the Church to contribute to building and increasing unity and to do our part to move the world towards a universal community.

Since this is our aim, you can see that it goes without saying that we are committed to creating and keeping up Christian relations of respect, trust and spiritual and practical help with all those who work with other Associations and Movements in the Catholic Church, whether it's at an international level or within the numerous nations where we are present.

We have a rich experience of working together with other Catholic Movements, at the request of the Church's authorities, in consultative bodies at many different levels, for pastoral councils, in an advisory capacity for the laity, for catechesis, for the family and for ecumenism. We have also worked together in other projects, as family counsellors, in centres for the protection of life, in courses for engaged couples and in many other activities at the specific request of the Church.

To give you an idea of our joining forces when we've worked together successfully with Catholic Action, Communion and Liberation, Opus Dei, the Pro-Life Movement and others, I could mention events like the Jubilee for the Family in 1984, the World Youth Day in the April of the same year and the World Youth Days at Buenos Aires and Santiago de Compostela. At present we are working together with others for the youth encounter at Czestochowa in August 1991.

To Each a Specific Gift

To sum up all these experiences, I would say that in the forty-seven years of the Movement's life we have seen that this collaboration between brothers and sisters, children of the same Mother Church is a typically Christian phenomenon.

At the same time, our years of experience have taught us that within the Church itself, each Movement should direct most of its time and energy to what its own charism and aims suggest. To do otherwise would be to betray its own vocation and neglect the purpose for which God called it into being, since each gift the Father gives to his Church is also a medicine for the whole of the mystical body which shouldn't be deprived of it. This is especially so for any era in which God has bestowed a particular gift, since it may be a means of strengthening and protecting Christians against the evils of the day.

I would also add that co-operation among Movements in the Church always bears fruit and never detracts from the specific task of each one, when it is requested or promoted by the central or local authority of the Church.

If this working together from time to time for specific purposes, in a joint effort towards commonly agreed objectives, and under the guidance of the Church's representatives, were to happen more frequently, possible prejudices would disappear of their own accord. Mutual respect and communion would increase, and the results would be unlike anything we have seen before, particularly from the point of view of the witness of unity that the world expects from Christians.

Which of the Movements you've mentioned does the Focolare feel closest to?

In our experience, even if there is a certain similarity between two Movements, this shouldn't be mistaken for a special relationship. There have been times during the development of the Movement when we have thought about a greater collaboration or even an amalgamation with some Movement similar to ours.

In the end, after the attempt was made with much good will on both sides, it resulted in nothing more than confusion for the members of both Movements. They were experiences that led to nothing and were a waste of time.

Despite their similarities, charisms are far more different from one another than you might imagine. I would repeat, however, that working together at the request of ecclesiastical authorities, for specific purposes and practical activities within set periods of time are not only useful but of great value.

Modern Scourges

Three ills of today's world are: its disintegration (in the break-down of social relations), escapism (into drugs, alcohol, violence) and consumerism (with its selfishness and the quest for pleasure). What answers do you suggest?

These ills of our world today are what happens when a culture and a society tear God out of the human heart, leaving behind a huge emptiness. Many substitutes are introduced to fill the void, but instead of making people happy, the results are devastating.

When a human being is separated from God, he is no longer really himself. He only finds himself again when he finds God. What happened in some Eastern European countries where nothing was spared to eradicate God from people's hearts is a clear example of this.

But how do you go about finding God again? We have seen that you have to invite people to come out of themselves, to start loving, because where there is love, there is God. The remedy for these sicknesses of today's society is the living of the Gospel, the Gospel of love. When it is lived, its effects are tangible; it produces works.

For almost fifty years now, both individual members and the various communities of the Movement spread throughout the world, have tried to respond in every possible way to this tendency towards fragmentation in society. There have already been achievements of different proportions, and often in the political and social hotbeds of the world most affected by social fragmentation, which have demonstrated the unifying and socializing effect of love, a turning away from the overriding influence of consumerism and a going against the tide in the drift towards hedonism and violence.

At a practical level, in 1990 alone, the Movement took on a range of commitments to aid the Lebanon, Panama, Eastern Europe, Iran and the Philippines after the earthquakes there. Following the Pope's appeal in February 1990, a project was launched in aid of the Sahel and is now fully operative.

'Open Hands'

For many years now, in a number of countries, our social projects have been tackling the problems caused by inequality between the rich and poor. This has been an ongoing operation, especially in countries where social deprivation is more evident.

In the North East of Brazil, in one of the poorest regions of the whole of South America, we have a project known as *Magnificat* working to improve and develop the agricultural activities of several rural communities. Despite the problems of an extremely difficult socio-economic situation, what *Magnificat* is achieving is highly significant. An experimental development programme based on the communion of goods has been successful both in the degree of participation by the poorer sections of the community and in the general improvements to their living standards. We believe it will be important also for the future of the region.

Another example of this is a project in the Philippines, in Manila. In Tagaytay, Cebu and Davao, there are social action centres known collectively as *Bukas Palad*, which means 'Open Hands', where rich and poor work together, in the unity that comes from mutual love and respect, in the running of a Health and Education programme with classes in literacy, hygiene and diet, as well as courses in general education.

There are many people who meet with others engaged in the same activities to share their experiences as doctors, artists, workers, politicians and so on, but many also meet together in the way I mentioned earlier on, in 'worlds', so as to build up a common approach that can go beyond the usual demarcations and conflicting positions. There are a great many teachers who, through an exchange of ideas, are devising a worldwide method of education for peace, valid for various age-groups and educational systems.

The Counter-Culture

As for escaping into drugs, alcohol and violence, our experience has shown us that this is often the result of a lack of ideals and values and of a feeling of loneliness.

We know that we have found a great ideal, and this is what we try to communicate. We want to respond to the wretchedness of loneliness by offering a life of communion. We have numerous projects to help drug addicts, alcoholics and gamblers. In Switzerland, for example, one group of Focolare members works with the drug addicts of Zurich's public park, the Platzspitz. Their relationship is based on actions rather than words and, with the co-operation of doctors and public bodies, many of those young people are being rehabilitated.

Finally, one tiny element of this counter-culture which is asserting itself amid the pressures of drugs, hedonism, escapism and violence is the ability of both young and old to exercise auto-censorship in T.V. viewing. All the members of the Movement of every age group are involved in a campaign to promote a mature and critical approach to television programming, so that it might become a means of information and growth.

'New Families'

Family life at present is undergoing a crisis of identity as a result of a variety of difficulties, including the tendency to deprive it of a role in society. How does this Movement of yours view and respond to this problem?

The Movement places a lot of value on its families, because we realize that while the family is now bearing the brunt of the storm, it is often by starting from the family that you can heal people and society.

This is the aim of the New Families Movement, a branch of the Focolare specifically concerned with the world of the family. Launched in 1967, it's now world-wide and has more than two hundred thousand members, as well as a vast circle of sympathizers whose exact numbers are difficult to ascertain. Igino Giordani, the first married Focolarino made a vital contribution to the foundation and growth of this Movement.

The New Families are concerned with promoting genuine values, and they have a widespread influence. Their witness to healthy family relationships, their openness to the society around them and their practice of decision-making in favour of life has had very positive results, such as reconciliations between family members of different generations and a recognition of the valuable contribution that the elderly have to make to family life.

Conferences, day meetings, formation courses, taking time off together, written publications and other means of communication are all avenues for their activities.

But above all, our families concentrate on living a life that is rooted in a personal choice of God, which each married partner makes independently as his or her personal response to God's personal love. As a result, the love between the couple and the love in the family is continuously revived and renewed, so Christ cannot but fulfil, also in the context of a family, his promise to be present among those who are united in his name. Igino Giordani used to say that the true vocation of a Christian family 'lies in keeping this flame alight at home and carrying its warmth outside the home into society, so that it too might become a family'.

The concern our families have for the society in which they live might be called 'their secret passion'. They see the moral disintegration of humanity and the tragic state of the family the world over as an image of the dying Christ as he cries out: 'My God, my God, why have you forsaken me?' They feel called to love in a special way those who belong to broken families, those who are alone, orphans, the handicapped, drug addicts, the old, the terminally ill, the marginalized and all the others who are in some way victims of our society.

By working to heal the family, the New Families are helping to achieve the aim of the entire Movement, which is the building of unity among all God's children. Families become strong through their lives in the Focolare and grow in faith to such an extent that sometimes they feel able to leave their own countries to go and live in other distant parts of the world to support our communities there. There are already more than one hundred families who have done this and they have become reference points for the whole Movement.

'Instalments' for Eastern Europe

We've seen walls, barriers and borders fall with breathtaking rapidity. Do the Focolarini see Eastern Europe as a field wide-open to the Gospel?

I should like to recall an event that has come to mind vividly again just recently. In 1961, two of us went to Hungary, one of the most troubled countries of Eastern Europe. The walls of the buildings still bore the stains and marks of the violent repression that had taken place, and you could feel the suspicion and fear in the air. There was a feeling of hopelessness which drowned all prospect of help and relief. We felt this as keenly as if we lived there ourselves.

When we discussed that terrible experience on our return to the Centre in Rome, we drew comfort and some shred of hope from an idea that began to take shape as we talked. We felt we wanted to do something to set the situation right, but we knew that such a grace could only be obtained at a high cost. We felt inadequate, but what we could do was to make contributions a little at a time. If here on earth you can buy a house, furniture or a car on the basis of instalments, could God be any less generous? We decided to offer our lives (when it pleased God to take them) as instalments to that end. Whenever any one of us left this life for heaven, and it was our practice to offer everything for the Church and the Movement, we would say, 'It's another instalment.' Perhaps this particular intention wasn't always foremost in our minds, but I'm sure God didn't forget it. And now God has answered—let's hope so anyway—those who did their part for the triumph of faith and freedom in many European countries and elsewhere, as well as the offering made by a thousand or so members the Movement who have died since 1960.

Over those years the spirituality of the Movement has spread to almost every country in Eastern Europe in unexpected and providential ways bringing comfort, joy and hope to so many people. So you see, the Focolarini have always had those countries and their troubled Churches very much in their hearts.

So what plans do you have in Eastern Europe?

We are sure that the Movement has a role of its own to play in Eastern Europe, where we already have several thousand members and adherents. We see that the people of those countries are divided roughly into two main groups. There are those who approve of freedom and are extremely happy to have finally achieved it, but there are also those who, while they know the past has gone, are nevertheless searching for a new way that will allow them to hold on to some of the things they believed in till now.

So what should our attitude be towards them both? With those who have found or rediscovered freedom, we should remember something which is equally true for the West and wherever there is freedom: that freedom isn't just a matter of choosing between good and evil; it's above all about continuously journeying towards goodness. It's this which makes you freer and freer. We'd like to emphasize too that freedom isn't about acquiring things, which is the case wherever consumerism rules, nor in searching for happiness at any price, which can lead to hedonism and drugs. Happiness is found in loving and in giving.

But most of all, we feel we really have to get down to loving by doing and by giving practical help to those whose task it is to build a new political, cultural and economic order for their countries. We have to support the Church there as it tries to improve its organization and strengthen itself. This is what we see as our job there.

What do you think about the fall of Marxism ?

First of all, you have to remember that the Marxist Movement couldn't have fascinated and attracted so many people and nations, if it hadn't been inspired by something worthwhile. Right from the start it offered new and powerful policies. It focussed on the disadvantaged classes deprived of human rights. It talked of unity with a global vision of the world and proclaimed peace as if it owned the rights to it. It raised awareness of the social reality of the human being and so on. These ideas or ideals were then largely ignored in what actually took place, but the ideas themselves existed and influenced and continue to influence those who believe in them. They shouldn't be destroyed, but, in order to avoid this, they have to be rooted in their original source, in God, in Jesus Christ. He more than anyone preferred the least, the poor. He made himself poor with them, and poorer than them when he died on the cross, completely stripped of every material and spiritual possession. He preached a society of communion, even modelling it on the life of the Holy Trinity which is complete communion. He was the personification of the truest and surest peace, and he lived so that there might be unity on earth, unity among people with all nations united as one. He lived for the unity of God's people, his Church which is called to be the sign and symbol of how the world should be.

We should keep this in mind and we believe that the Focolare Movement does have something to say on this subject, and Eastern Europe would seem to be a place that is particularly suited to our sort of evangelization.

We know that many people in Eastern Europe are feeling lost and bewildered at the speed of events taking place there. They feel deeply disillusioned and depressed at seeing the ideals, in which they had believed in all good faith, being smashed to pieces.

So while we share the joy and commitment of those who are moving towards a different sort of future in their newly found freedom, we would also like to be beside these others to assure them that all is not lost, that God can draw out good from everything, that he follows the course of history and has surely followed theirs, that unity is possible and that their dream can yet become a marvellous reality, not through hatred and conflict but with love, with God.

In Africa

You've explained what the Focolarini throughout the world have in common, but how do they differ from one another? For example, the idea of 'focolare', of family life,[41] varies from culture to culture. For Africans the family always has a strong ancestral and tribal significance. Is this reflected in some way in the organization?

Since you mention the Africans, I can tell you that our experience in Africa is an example of inculturation in a context that is very different from the one in which the Movement first began. It all started in 1963 when Bishop Peeters of the Buea diocese in Cameroon invited us over, because he was convinced that this spirit was what was needed for the young Church there. Within a few months, some Focolarini, three men, two of whom were doctors and another a veterinary surgeon, and three women, left for Cameroon. After an initial period of settling in and getting to know both the missionary situation and medical practice in a missionary environment, these men and women Focolarini were invited to set up their communities in a region that hadn't yet been evangelized. The bishop said, 'Yours is a new spirituality, so you should start your experience from zero in a completely new place.'

This is how they found themselves in Fontem, a remote region of forest and of savanna, with a hot and humid climate and eight to ten months of rain during the year. This region of country was inhabited by a tribe of about twenty thousand people, threatened with extinction because of their extreme isolation and because of common tropical diseases, such as sleeping sickness and filariasis.

The head of the tribe, the Fon of Fontem, had made repeated appeals in vain to the government and to the various Churches. In a final attempt to get help, he made a collection among his people to put together a sum of money and set off with a delegation to meet the Catholic

Bishop, to whom he made the following speech: 'We have come to realize that God is not answering our prayers, because we are too wicked. We have brought you this money and would like you to make all your Christians pray for us. Perhaps God will listen to them!' I think we can say that God answered their prayers by sending the Focolarini to Fontem.

Now twenty seven years have passed and the Movement has spread to many countries in Africa. Fontem itself has expanded and many of our members work there. What was once a place lost in the forest is now a small town and even something more than that. You could say, in fact, that what happened in Fontem was a completely new experience for us. Not only did the Movement develop with all its structures, but the numerous conversions to Christianity as a result of loving without any such expectations meant that the local Church began to spring up and take root.

Now, to go back to your question, it is obvious that the same ideas and truths (and I include 'Focolare' in this) are received and interpreted in a different way in African culture, as they are in fact in every culture.

With its spirituality which is universal and its uncomplicated and adaptable structures, the Movement has managed to integrate itself in an African context without altering its own identity at all.

In Africa as elsewhere, we have tried to be authentic witnesses to Christ and this has led thousands of people to him. We have also been able to establish very deep relationships built on charity with many people who remain outside of the institutional Church for reasons such as polygamy.

When the African Focolarini share their experiences of living the Gospel with us, we are always struck by their simple evangelical attitude and by the particular beauty of their African identity.

Yes, it's true that the African focolares are different from other focolares in other countries and cultures, but the substance is the same because there is a single spirit in them all. However, that very same way of living, that very same light, which is the presence of Jesus in his people and among his people, highlights the most precious values to be found in Africa, which together with all other cultures form the colourful composition of a redeemed humanity.

Four Kinds of Dialogue

The religious world both inside and outside of Christianity goes through various crises. The same is true of the secular world. Where does the Movement stand with regard to these worlds and what contribution does it make to solve their problems?

It's not such a great leap to make from the problems of a little town like Trent to the great world crises, because the way of responding to them doesn't change. The importance and the extent of the help you have to offer may change with the years, but the motive from the beginning has always been, and continues to be, the desire to fulfil Jesus' testament: 'Father, may they all be one'. Yes, this is what we live for. Even if it might seem over-ambitious, it's this will, the last will of Jesus that we want to make our own. He was the one to put it in our hearts.

But what has unity, Jesus' testament, got to do with the problems of today's world? I believe that the deepest aspiration of humanity is the desire for unity, for love. At the same time it's also humanity's greatest problem. When there is no love, the element of cohesion between individuals, groups and nations is destroyed. The wars, hunger, poverty and suffering which result are nothing less than the face of disunity.

But how is unity created? Paul VI spoke of an indispensable means to this end. It's dialogue, and the Movement has used this means, in its own way, right from the beginning.

The Movement is engaged in four main areas of dialogue. There's the dialogue within the Catholic world where the Movement makes its contribution to enable the Church to become always more one in itself. There is the dialogue in the wider Christian world to contribute to its unification. There's the dialogue in the world of other religions, so that, getting to know and respect one another more, we might witness to and make known the God of Jesus Christ. Finally, in the secular world, there's a dialogue of working together with all of good will, where we work to build, consolidate and extend the universal family.

How would you describe the Movement's ecumenism and its relationship with members of other Churches?

The ecumenical activity of the Focolare Movement lies both in helping Catholics to become more aware of Christian unity and more committed to it, as well as in its efforts to create Christian communion with members of all the different Churches.

About thirty-six thousand people from two hundred and twenty Churches (Evangelicals, Anglicans, Reformed Church members etc.) have welcomed our spirituality, and many of them are involved in the life and activities of the Movement.

A Wonderful Atmosphere

So ecumenism was one of Chiara Lubich's early intuitions, but why do you think the leaders of Christian denominations other than your own were so open and welcoming to you?

A young man who happened to be present at one of the youth meetings organized by the Gen wrote down his impressions on a piece of paper before he left, and I think his words might supply the answer to your question. He said: 'God is love, and you have shown this to me.' It seems that watching all the young people of his age who were united together there, he became aware of the presence of Another, of God who is Love present in their midst. More than anything else, it is this unity which has opened doors into other Churches and denominations.

There are enormous possibilities for unity with other Churches. We share the same baptism, believe in the same Gospel, the same Christ, the same Holy Spirit, and our spirituality highlights all of these. They too want to put the new commandment of Jesus into practice, so we live it together with them. The consequences of this are great. Jesus is present among us and we can witness to him together. This witness has been verified time and time again during the history of the Movement. Just one example of this was during the early sixties. We had got to know some Evangelicals in Germany, and we had started holding meetings for Evangelicals and Catholics in Rome. I remember that at one meeting, which was blessed with great joy and seemed to go particularly well, there were also three Anglicans present. They remarked on 'the wonderful atmosphere' they had found between Catholics and Lutherans. The following year they came back with a hundred others, and that's how the Movement started among Anglicans.

What makes you and the faithful of other Churches who share the spirituality of unity, so keen to pursue this dialogue and so committed day by day to building up all the communion which is now possible? And what difficulties have you met with in your approach to ecumenism?

The explanation for all of this lies in one name: Jesus crucified and forsaken. On the cross, he experienced the greatest separation you could imagine. Although he was God, in some way he experienced disunity from the Father, and yet he overcame it saying: 'Father, into your hands I commit my spirit.'[42]

Whenever we are together as Catholics with Evangelicals, or whenever Evangelicals or Anglicans are together with Catholics, it's not long before we feel that something is wrong which prevents there being the fullness of unity. Our different histories and cultures have given us different outlooks, and this can hurt and make us suffer. But then we remember Jesus forsaken and try to do as he did, by loving this suffering, by going beyond it. It is only when we go beyond the suffering and reach peace and joy that we can carry on loving the others. Our strength comes from looking at him and doing what he did.

We have always recognized Jesus forsaken in the Christian world which is called to the most perfect unity and is now subdivided into hundreds of different Churches. It's because of him, because of his cry that rises up from so many traumatic situations, divisions and separations, that we feel committed to working for the rebuilding of unity in the Church.

It's because of him that we have been able to get to know so many Churches and Christian confessions, to understand and appreciate their special characteristics and to discover that we are members of the same Christian family through our shared baptism and our mutual evangelical love. It's because of him that we shall never give up, even when the going is hard.

The Golden Rule

Another sphere of the Movement's activity is its dialogue with other religions. Why do you think the spiritual leaders and the ordinary followers of other religions have listened to the Movement and established warm ties with it?

The Second Vatican Council said that the Holy Spirit 'calls all to Christ through the seeds of the Word and the preaching of the Gospel'.[43] I think this explains a little why the spirituality of the Movement has had such a strong influence on members of other faiths.

The first thing we do is to announce the Gospel by living it. The members of other faiths are extremely sensitive to genuine spiritual values. Their religious traditions contain truths and seeds of the Word which prepare them for the message of the Gospel.

But above all, what brings our dialogue alive is the fact that our spirituality and witness is centred on love, which calls forth an immediate and spontaneous response in everybody, no matter what their religion is, because you can find this 'golden rule' of doing to others what you would have them do to you in all religions.[44] There is a 'way of love which is open to everybody',[45] as the Council stated, which is the work of the Holy Spirit who operates beyond the visible boundaries of the Church.

We have seen that if we try to live this evangelical love among ourselves and with everyone, when we come to speak with our friends of other religions, we find that they are very open indeed. They believe in love, because they have seen it in action in our focolares, in the little towns and in the Mariapolises.

In your interfaith dialogue, have you found any common ground or any similarities that enable you to build bridges with other religions?

I would love to tell you at length about what we have discovered in common and what draws us together. We have realized for example that the suffering which Jesus experienced, which led to his complete destruction in the suffering of the abandonment, is a source of deep fascination for Eastern religions. In fact, it is often through a mortification of the senses and every desire that they seek that 'energy' (which is how they call it) which is sustained by God, who they frequently love as a person. Their asceticism is to be admired; it draws them to such heights that they acquire a certain understanding of the supernatural life of the Christian when they come into contact with genuine Christians. It is the reality of 'being' which has significance for them. When someone dies to himself or herself to become one with them, thus allowing Christ to live in the self, or when they come into contact with the Risen Christ among Christians who are united, in itself a fruit of loving the cross, they are able to recognize that light, that peace which comes from the Spirit which is evident on people's faces, and they are attracted by it and ask for it to be explained to them. It is at this point that we speak of our religion and enter into a dialogue which becomes evangelization.

Some Buddhist philosophers told us that the Christian's renunciation of self in the imitation of Jesus' kenosis on the cross, as the Movement presents it, is very close to the perfection of the void of Buddhism.

Buddhist compassion manifest in practical service for the good of humanity is also very close to Christian love. Their work for world peace has won our support and collaboration in projects such as the World Conference for Religion and Peace (WCRP) to which the Movement has made a notable contribution.

To sum up, I would say that, in these few years of interfaith dialogue, we have developed all the various lines of dialogue outlined in the Church's official pronouncements. Hence, there is the 'dialogue of life' carried out in everyday contacts with people of other religions; there is the 'dialogue of action' in working together in the various international and interfaith organizations; there is the 'dialogue of experts' led by members of the Movement who have studied the various traditions and religions; and there is the 'dialogue of religious experience' in which we share our living experience in the light of our respective Holy Writings and traditions.

What has surprised us is the number of Buddhists, Muslims, Jews, Hindus and followers of other religious traditions (about twenty thousand or so) who have wanted to belong to the Movement and to live as far as is possible for them, the same spirituality as we do, working together for a united world.

And finally on the subject of dialogues, would I be right in saying that the Movement has a special commitment to dialogue with the secular world or better with people who used to be referred to as atheists?

Yes, we feel that this is a very important aspect of our dialogue. Even from the outset it was love for Jesus crucified and forsaken that spurred us towards people who in many different ways were estranged from God, at least in their beliefs. Experience has shown us, however, how thirsty these people are for God and how much openness of mind there actually is among some who might be described as atheists.

In recent years, this dialogue has made considerable progress, and deep relationships have flourished throughout the world with many self-proclaimed atheists and agnostics, as well as with numbers of people who have left off practising their faith for years or who are indifferent to it. Many of them are impressed by the way the members of the Movement live. They are intrigued and interested and often want to know what lies behind the way of life they see practised. They begin to come to some of our meetings and there they encounter solidarity, equality, unity and peace, all of which are ideals to which many of them had long aspired. Moreover, they see that all of this is a result of the Gospel put into practice and, while some rediscover their faith, others find it for the first time. Our records show that about ninety-six thousand such people are in contact with us of whom more than twenty-two thousand take part in our activities.

VII

Encounters

'You are the Daughter of two Fathers'

You have held and continue to hold conversations with the great religious figures of our times. One such relationship was with Athenagoras I, the Ecumenical Patriarch of Constantinople. How did this come about and what insights did you gain from it?

I remember that the first time I met with Patriarch Athenagoras was in June 1967 at the invitation of some mutual friends. When I told him something of my aspirations, of the work for Christian unity, he found a striking similarity between what I was telling him and what he himself felt about these things and he said to me, 'You are my daughter! You have two fathers: a great one in Rome, Paul VI (whom he regarded as a second St Paul), and another, an old one, in me, here.' Both then and at other times, he spoke of the Pope in a way I have never heard from another. His personal love for the Pope was evident in his solicitude for the smallest details concerning him. For example, he would say to me, 'Tell him to eat more, to go for walks sometimes and to get some fresh air.'

He always used to read the *Osservatore Romano* so he was familiar with all the Pope's talks. He used to say that whatever Paul VI was doing, he was doing it to-gether with him. When the Pope was on one of his journeys, Athenagoras would say to me, 'I was there too, I was there with him.' This accompanying of the Pope was more real to him than the fact he was in Istanbul, but it was a spiritual closeness, a supernatural one which is stronger than a natural presence.

Caviar from the Patriarch

What I learnt from Athenagoras was not only this extremely sensitive love for the Pope, I also learnt about the quality of charity that must always take priority over any conversation we might be planning. We never got down to talking before he had offered, and I had ac-cepted, some gesture of hospitality such as a coffee. He wanted to pay for the hotel I stayed in, because he wanted me to be his guest. At the Fanar where we would meet, there was always a room prepared with the great-est attention for me to dine in. Even on the days when the Orthodox were fasting and abstaining, he did not want to inconvenience me in any way and so for me there was. . . caviar.

But in addition to these tiny details, I saw the great love he had for all peoples. During his long life he had got to know many and knew how to see goodness everywhere. I do not know how he did it, but I am sure he had a very special gift in this regard. From him I learnt to love all nations, to find the good in them all. He never had a bad word for any of them. Athenagoras was truly great; it would be impossible to forget him. It was he who showed us the beauty of the Orthodox Church, and from him too we understood how important it is in the Eastern Churches to translate truth into life and to exalt love.

My relationship with the Patriarch was a deep one, due partly to the fact that he knew Paul VI so well. Since I had personal contact with the Holy Father, I found myself acting as a means through which the Patriarch could communicate informally with the Pope.

Athenagoras longed to re-establish full communion with the Catholic Church after a thousand years of separation, and I used to find myself recording his sentiments, his thoughts and his hopes and conveying them to Pope Paul VI. I believe this role of mine was important in helping to consolidate the unity between these two Church leaders. Paul VI had enormous respect for the Patriarch and on hearing of his death he said, 'A saint has died.'

Dimitrios I, the successor to Athenagoras, is also interested in the development of the Movement.[46]

Which other religious leaders have given you stimulus and spiritual enrichment?

I have been able to have personal contact with the last three leaders of the Church of England: Michael Ramsey, Donald Coggan and Robert Runcie. They all gave me a warm welcome and the relationship developed into a sincere friendship.

Michael Ramsey, who received me at Lambeth Palace in London, immediately recognized 'the hand of God in this Movement' and encouraged me to work to 'build a spiritual communion with them so that hearts might be warmed by this spirit'. The Movement spread throughout the Anglican world, because of the support given by these leaders.

In 1962, in Munich, I spoke with the then President of the Council of the Evangelical Church in Germany, Dr Dietzfelbinger. It was my first venture into ecumenism and I was deeply impressed by his openness. This occasion and further meetings with him saw a new development of the Movement in Germany. The Catholic Bishop, Bishop J. Stimpfle was joined by Dr Dietzfelbinger in the joint blessing of Ottmaring Centre, which is a ecumenical little town near Augsburg where Catholics and Evangelicals share their lives together.

Further relationships of this kind have developed with other Evangelical leaders, as indeed with leaders of other Churches.

Dialogue with Buddhism in Japan

In your book, 'Meetings with the East',[47] you write about your experiences with the great religious traditions there and also about your personal relationship with a Japanese Buddhist leader, Nikkyo Niwano. Can you tell me something about him, about your impressions, the results of your conversations and what you have learnt about interfaith dialogue?

I remember our first meeting very well. It was at the beginning of 1979, when we were waiting for a clear sign, for some way to open up so that we could develop this new dialogue which attracted us so strongly. A variety of circumstances prepared the way for my first meeting with Nikkyo Niwano, but the final thing was his nomination for the Templeton Prize in 1979. He had to visit Italy and asked if we could meet. It wasn't merely an interest in meeting a former prize winner.

Already in Japan, in the United States and in Italy some of the young people from the Rissho Kosei-kai, the Buddhist organization he founded, had met up with our own young people. We had been struck by their freshness, their openness and their smiles, and they had returned to Japan impressed by our spirituality and the life they had found in the groups they had visited.

But there was another much earlier event that drew us together, which I only became aware of when I got to know him better. An incident that had deeply influenced his whole life was his meeting with Paul VI during the Vatican Council in 1964. He spoke of that meeting with awe, because it was then he had understood that he had to dedicate his whole life to a greater understanding between the religions of the East and the West. Just a few years later, his efforts led to the founding of the World Conference for Religion and Peace, of which he became honorary president. This conference has made him become well-known in international religious circles.

When I met him, my immediate feeling was that we were made to work together, because his organization and the Focolare Movement had much in common. He clearly felt the same way and invited me to speak about my religious experience to the leaders of his organization at an event I referred to earlier in this interview.

And then in Tokyo we had a second and a third meeting. I remember feeling so free with him and of being able to speak openly of my Christian faith; I think we spoke of little else other than of Jesus. The truth is that an opening had been made for me because of the witness of Gospel life seen in the Movement's communities which had so deeply impressed the youth of the Rissho Kosei-kai and Nikkyo Niwano himself.

During those conversations I understood quite clearly that a real dialogue could now get under way and that the dialogue itself could become a form of evangelization. The Holy Spirit had prepared us for this by teaching us above all to love, to make ourselves one with the other person, to transform suffering into love, into joy.

With these ideas alone, I knew that we would be able to converse with Buddhists, for instance, about their four noble truths to extinguish suffering, and it was as if I could see a way being prepared for the proclamation of Christ and of Christ Crucified, of the One who went to the cross in order to conquer suffering and death.

But Buddhists have to experience this Jesus in some way; they have to touch him in us Christians, and this can only happen when in us there is something of Christ's own love, that love which makes us ready to give our lives for others.

So what were my impressions of Nikkyo Niwano? I spoke about them to a Japanese journalist who interviewed me during my stay there. I said that it was impossible to remain untouched by that unfailing smile; the smile of a profoundly spiritual person who is guided from within by a pure and sensitive conscience. I found in him someone who was wise, attentive and constantly listening to God's Spirit.

In 1985, I was once again invited by the president Niwano to the celebration of his sanju, his eightieth birthday. It was his wish that I be one of the official speakers at the event in the Great Sacred Hall in Tokyo where I addressed a gathering of thousands of representatives from religious, cultural and political bodies in Japan.

I remember how surprised and moved my Catholic friends and I were when we listened to the talk he gave in the afternoon to the assembled Buddhist youth. He suggested that should their consciences urge them to become Christians, then they should do so, expressing in this way his respect and love both for the Pope and for the Catholic Church.

'I'm not the Only One Who's Mad'

During that visit we were able to review together how much we had managed to work together and, more importantly, to have a deep spiritual sharing.

He spoke enthusiastically of his great hope in young people. Even at his age he was still young at heart, because he was open to the highest realms of the spirit. At one point in tones that were prophetic, he said, 'If we are united and act in accordance with the will of God, soon there will be peace in the world. I have dedicated myself to this cause for many years. . .' He then added jokingly, 'I thought I was the only one who's mad and doing this, until I met you.'

He then gave me a gift of a fan which had, written on it in Chinese characters, the words of a revered Buddhist monk who lived eleven centuries ago. Nikkyo explained their meaning to me, 'If my heart is one with the will of God, it will see thousands of other hearts coming to life around it.'

That meeting in November '85 was the last conversation I had with him, because I had to return to Rome sooner than I had originally planned when the Holy Father invited me to be an observer at the Synod of Bishops.

Soon afterwards Nikkyo Niwano suggested we continue this exchange of our thoughts through letters. It's a way to examine contemporary topics, such as ecology and peace. He writes to me as a Buddhist with all the wealth of his spiritual experience, and I reply on the same topic offering my own beliefs and pointing out what we share in common as well as what is new and specific to the Christian view of these things. And so this dialogue continues even at a distance.

VIII

In Conversation with Popes

'The Church Needs What You Have!'

Recent Popes have expressed their appreciation of your work. Could you tell me about your meetings with them, starting with Pius XII?

We had an audience with Pope Pius XII, in the Vatican, on 21 May 1953. When we were presented to him, the Holy Father immediately made it clear that he knew of us. He said, 'Ah, the Focolare. Good, very good! Where's the one behind it all?' He turned to me, with the tenderness of a father towards his child, and enquired about what each one of us did and where we came from. We explained that we represented various regions in Italy where the Movement had spread.

The Pope was particularly interested in Tuscany and Emilia explaining that the effects of materialism were more evident in areas where communism was more widespread.

'We want to bring Jesus to the world', said one of our group, 'and each one of us represents hundreds of others who are closely linked to us. . . . We want to give joy to the Church.'

'And the Church is greatly in need of it', replied the Pope. He continued, 'Keep up this fervour. Go forward!'

At the end of our conversation, he gave us his special blessing and as he moved away from our group, his eyes continued to follow us. We all felt that there was something very special in the fatherly recognition he had shown us.

We did not have any special meetings with Pope John XXIII, but it was during his pontificate that the Focolare Movement was approved by the Holy See as a Work by pontifical right.

'Here Everything is Possible'

What was your relationship with Paul VI like?

We got to know Paul VI when he was Monsignor Montini of the Secretariat of State. We used to keep him informed on the development of the Movement and its spirituality. He was very interested in it and used to make suggestions and give us valuable advice.

When he became Pope, I had several audiences with him. He always wanted to know what was going on in the Movement. We had been approved, but the juridical aspect fell somewhat short of our expectations. I told him about this, because he encouraged me to to tell him everything, explaining 'because here everything is possible!' Shortly afterwards, he himself intervened on our behalf to get the Statutes altered.

In another audience with him, I told him about the participation of Christians other than Catholics in our Movement. I spoke, for example, about how in Germany I had met with Lutheran bishops, several pastors and many lay people who were not particularly sympathetic towards the Catholic Church but who had welcomed the spirituality of the Movement. I said how they had accepted our invitation to come to Rome and to participate in general audiences with Pope John and in his own general audiences, where they had been deeply impressed by what they had seen.

I also told him about other meetings that had taken place in Germany with Evangelicals and Lutherans who had invited us to speak about our Movement and about how, in explaining our spirituality, we were able to talk openly about Mary and also about the Pope and that they had been happy about this.

The Pope listened to all I said in deep silence. These subjects seemed to interest him a great deal, so much so that when I had finished, he told me that it was the will of God for us to take a special interest in this ecumenical dialogue, as well as in the dialogue we had begun with non-believers both in the West and in Eastern European countries.

In that same audience, he entrusted us with a special apostolic mission. He explained how Christianity was still alive in some Eastern European countries, but that little information could be obtained. He suggested that it would be a magnificent work of charity if we could set up something to do with tourism which could be a means of bringing spiritual comfort to people in those countries, as well as a way to approach and befriend visitors who came to the West.

I agreed immediately to his suggestion and shortly afterwards we set up a centre called 'Incontri Romani'[48] in which a group of Focolarini who spoke both Eastern and Western European languages dedicated themselves to this particular activity.

I also remember that sometime during this same meeting, the Pope remarked in unequivocal terms that our Movement was a 'Work of God' and just before he gave me his blessing at the end, he said, 'If ever you have something to tell me personally then come and I will see you immediately.'

On another occasion when I spoke with him, he continued to repeat that the Movement was a majestic Work, like a volcano because of its many different dimensions and expressions, each one more splendid than the next. He said that it needed to be given the chance to flourish in all its vastness, in all its fullness. He also added, 'You are people of the Council.'

In subsequent years, many different groups from the Movement who were taking part in meetings at the Mariapolis Centre in Rocca di Papa, would attend Pope Paul VI's general audiences. These Wednesday appointments became a tradition and have remained as landmarks in the life of the whole Movement.

We collected together the words Paul VI addressed to our various groups in the years 1965 to 1978 in a book entitled: 'Paul VI to the Focolare Movement',[49] so that this precious legacy of encouragement, direction and instruction could always remain alive for us.

'You Can Tell Who They Are'

We'll have to allow plenty of space for John Paul II. The Pope is your friend. He said so himself at the last Genfest. But what were your impressions when you met him for the first time? What did he say to you?

It has been an immense grace to have known the Pope personally and to have met with him on various occasions in private audiences, working breakfasts and dinners, at the Movement's large scale events and on his visits to our Centres.

Right from the very first audience, I had the wonderful impression of a Pope who listens to you, a Pope who is attentive and sensitive and who is not satisfied with a superficial acquaintance. He asked me questions and wanted to know in detail about our spirituality, about the spread of the Movement throughout the world. It was not necessary to say a lot. Just a word or a mention of something, and you felt understood in a way that no one else in the world is able to make you feel. You could sense the charism of Peter in an almost tangible way, in a completely unique way, and then it would be he who would speak about your own charism, placing it in God's plan of salvation for our world today.

This first impression has been reconfirmed and reinforced over the years, as I have marvelled at the amazing way he gives himself to the Church and to each individual. That's how he has been with us too. Those who have participated in any of the hundreds of public and private audiences in the Sala Nervi or at Castel Gandolfo, share the same experience of feeling personally loved by him, but loved for themselves, as people, as Christians and, I have to say, loved as members of the Focolare Movement. So many times, he himself has told me about meeting groups of Focolarini or Gen in different parts of the world. 'You can tell who they are,' he says with a smile.

The Pope has visited the headquarters of the Focolare several times and he has also been to some of your large scale events. Can you tell me about those occasions?

Perhaps the most delightful visit was the one that was both unplanned and exceptional, when he came to our centre at Rocca di Papa. Because our International Centre is close to Castel Gandolfo, we were always hesitant about inviting him as we were reluctant to deprive him of any rare chance he has to get some rest. And so he invited himself on 19 August 1984, a day we regard as one of the most beautiful the Movement has experienced.

It was an exceptional day, not only because that's how he described it himself, but exceptional and unforgettable in that the Pope spoke to us of our ecclesial and spiritual identity. There were three thousand of us waiting for him on the spacious lawns in front of the Centre, and it was a wonderful celebration that lasted several hours.

Since then he has addressed almost every large scale event the Movement has organized, when he has given not only words of encouragement and advice but, way and above formal protocol, has also expressed his warmest friendship and personal affection for each and every one of the participants, which, needless to say, has always been reciprocated with explosive enthusiasm from the thousands of young people present, as well as the not quite so young.

I could tell you about the 1980 Genfest held in the Flaminio Stadium, Rome, and later in St Peter's Square and the 1990 Genfest held in Rome's Paleur, all occasions that were enriched by his presence, his attentiveness and his words.

Among the events the Pope has attended have been the large gatherings of the New Families Movement (Paleur 1981), the New Humanity Movement (Paleur 1985), the International Congress of the priests and religious of the Movement, in 1982 in the Pope Paul VI Hall, when the Pope's concelebrated mass with seven thousand priests was described by the *Osservatore Romano* as 'a historic event'. He was also present for the International Congress of the Parishes Movement in the Pope Paul VI Hall in 1986.

When the Audience Hall at Castel Gandolfo became our Mariapolis Centre after the Pope spontaneously suggested that we acquire it for our use, his visits took on an informal family-like tone, because of the easy access he had to the centre from his residence and because of the warmth of the talks he gave when he came.

His first visit at the end of '86 was like an inauguration of the new Centre and, on his latest visit, in 1989, he stayed to breakfast with some of the leaders of the Movement, after he had celebrated mass for the one thousand two hundred people in the various groups who were meeting that day at the Centre.

A Very Simple Charism

What are the most important things the Pope has said in his talks to the Focolarini?

We were particularly touched by what he said during his visit to the Movement's International Centre at Rocca di Papa.

Some of the Movement's leaders together with myself gave a brief presentation of the Movement's spirit and its structures, and then the Pope began to speak. What he said was quite spontaneous, but it will always be like a point of reference for us. He said, 'Yours is a new charism, a charism for our times, a charism which is both very simple and attractive because the simplest and most compelling thing in our religion is charity. It's the heart of Christianity, the heart of the Gospel. But this charity, this love isn't an easy thing. In fact, it is extremely difficult and demanding . . .'

Then referring to the ecumenical contacts we have built with many Christian Churches and the dialogue we have with non-Christians and non-believers, the Pope said, 'The very structure of the Movement itself almost reflects the vision, the ecclesiology of Vatican II. The charism of your Movement is Vatican II interpreted with your experience, with your apostolate, with this vital principle of yours.'

At the end of the meeting he said, 'I have seen how the Movement lives and grows throughout the world as it accomplishes its mission . . . In today's world, in the life of nations, in different societies, in different environments and in individuals, hatred and conflict are both part and parcel of the agenda. What is needed is love, what is needed is an agenda of love . . . And this is what your faith is; it's the inspiring spark of all that is done in the name of Focolare . . . You must keep to this same path. You already have your own quite distinct course, your own clear identity, your own charism, in the abundance of love which comes from God himself, from the Holy Spirit . . . Your aim is to bring radical, evangelical love to the lives of all people throughout the world, and you give witness to God who is love.'[50]

As you can imagine, these words of the Pope have remained etched in our hearts. On the other occasions when he has addressed us, he has repeatedly confirmed the spiritual direction of the Movement and the particular activity of each branch of the Movement, emphasizing the coherence to the Gospel and fidelity to the Church which motivate it and underlie its activities.

Each time we hear him speak, we thank God for the exceptional gift of discernment he has given to the Pope and for this loving service of 'encouraging the brethren'.

Finally, I should like to make brief mention of a few words he addressed to us one Sunday in May '86, when more than seven thousand of our members had just had an audience with him. It was the moment of the Angelus and the Pope was at his window looking out over St Peter's Square and, perhaps, he had been moved by the spiritual atmosphere he had encountered. He began the Angelus by addressing Mary as 'Mother of the Focolare, Mary of the Focolarini'.

In John Paul II's own teaching, what has most impressed and inspired you?

I have to mention a particular aspect of John Paul II's teaching that I think is both original and typical of him.

His modern approach and openness to both the long-standing and the newer problems of the world is well-known, as is his personal and profound competence in the sphere of dogmatic and moral theology. To my mind, however, his greatest achievement is in the area of ecclesiology. He is known, for instance, for his insistence on the need to make the sacramental and juridical nature of communion, a living reality. For example, when he addressed a gathering of bishops who are linked with us as friends of the Movement, he invited them to transform effective collegiality, that is, juridical collegiality, into an affective one since it is love that is the principle of the trinitarian communion on which the Church is founded.

Another great innovation the Pope has promoted during these ten years of his pontificate is something that emerged from Vatican II and is scripturally based. It is the Church's new self-awareness of its complementary Marian and Petrine dimensions.

I was deeply moved when I read a passage addressed some years ago to the Roman Curia in which he underlined the Marian profile of the Church declaring it to be 'just as fundamental and characteristic as the apostolic and Petrine profile, if not more so'.

In fact, he asserted that 'the Marian dimension of the Church precedes the Petrine, while being closely bound and complementary to it' and that the Marian profile of the Church comes first in God's plan as it did, in fact, in a historical sense and is, moreover, superior to it, with a richer significance both for the individual and for the community.[51]

I remember writing several years ago that 'only Mary understands the Church and only the Church understands Mary'. The 'totus tuus' the Pope addresses to Mary is not a mere figure of speech for him, it's the code by which he lives. It explains his Marian personality, his greatness, his human sensitivity. It elevates him and at the same time brings him to the level of all, a man among many, a genuine 'servant of the servants of God', with an awareness of his own Petrine charism and free of all trace of clericalism.

Operation Bricks

The Pope put the audience Hall at Castel Gandolfo at the disposal of the Movement. How did this come about?

Yes, it was an exceptional gift. You would have a better idea of our joy and gratitude if you knew the situation we were in at that time on 5 December 1982, the day the Holy Father put the audience Hall of Castel Gandolfo at our disposal.

I even wrote about it to the Pope. I wanted to tell him how indescribably happy we were and that we had been a little like Mary and Joseph looking for shelter in Bethlehem, because the accommodation we could provide at our little Mariapolis Centre in Rocca di Papa had become completely inadequate for the numbers of people who were coming to our meetings. Providence had brought us this exceptional gift.

We had secretly hoped to build one day what we described as a Cathedral to Jesus present among us, in other words, a building that would be dedicated by and to his presence, which is the only purpose of our meetings. It would have had to take into consideration the scale of the Movement today, and it is clear to me that our Father in heaven lent us a hand, as we would never have found the place and the means to build something like that.

Naturally, this big hall had to be turned into something more serviceable so we were looking at a substantial amount of money. That is when Operation Bricks began, which turned out to be an amazing feat of generosity throughout the whole Movement. Everyone, from the smallest to the oldest gave what they had according to their means. Finding all the money needed for the construction work was the second miracle which enabled us to start the work and carry it through to completion.

We are immensely grateful to God, the Holy Father and all those who raised the money brick by brick, as well as all the technicians in the Movement who worked at every stage in the planning and the eventual construction of a building that reflects the style and the aims of the Movement itself.

My Superior is the Pope

Personally speaking, what do you feel you owe to John Paul II?

As you know well by now, I am not comfortable speaking specifically about myself, but this is one of the rare times when I feel I ought to in order to tell you what I owe to John Paul II.

When you are with him, you really feel you can be yourself, because he loves you for yourself, for the charism you perhaps have, for the service you give to the Church; he loves the Movement that has come to life because of the charism, both for what it is and for what it does. He makes you feel that, as a woman, you are the heart of humanity; a daughter, yes, but also a co-worker in helping the Church grow together into communion.

This is what I have experienced in my contacts with him and it is also why I recognize his greatness. John Paul II does not differentiate between men and women. He loves and highlights the charisms in both. In women he sees Mary, the masterpiece of creation, but he also knows that woman is a masterpiece if she is truly woman. What I mean is that he does not regard the Marian profile of the Church just as a spiritual or mystical reality, but as a historical phenomenon and he follows this through in his actions. He knows for example that our Movement is called 'Work of Mary', and he never fails to emphasize its Marian presence in the Church.

I also have to say, even though it's quite personal and intimate, that my superior is the Pope. In my conversations with him, I try to live at the deepest possible level, my own unity and the unity of the whole Movement with the one who represents God and the Church for me. In this way we are nothing other than Church within the Church. If I did not have this unity which is a personal unity with the Holy Father, I could not live unity and could not represent it within the Movement itself.

When I meet with him, something happens which does not happen in my relationship with anyone else. I experience a deep union with God, the only one of its kind. It is something that lasts for varying lengths of time, but it gives me strength, joy and comfort to take up my task in the Movement in a completely new way.

A Privileged Channel

What importance does the Pope give to the Focolare Movement in the present day Church scenario?

First of all, I would widen this question to all the new ecclesial Movements and the role they play in the Church. John Paul II, as you know, has a high regard for the Movements because, and I read a passage from his own talk on this subject, 'they are founded on the charismatic gifts that together with the hierarchical gifts . . . constitute those gifts with which the Holy Spirit has adorned the Church, the bride of Christ'.[52]

He says that they are distinct gifts 'but also mutually complementary'. Fearing not to have been sufficiently explicit, he adds that 'in the Church, the charismatic aspect as much as the institutional aspect, the Movements of the faithful and associations as much as the hierarchy, are co-essential and together contribute to life, renewal and sanctification'. And since the Movements try to live the Word of God in the real situations of history, 'with their very witness, they bring evangelical life to the contemporary affairs and values of humanity and enrich the Church with a boundless and endless variety of activities in the spheres of charity and holiness'.

The Holy Father is convinced that the phenomenon of the Movements 'has and will have great importance in the future of the Church' precisely because he sees 'in the new lay charisms, the key to the vital insertion of the Church in the historical context of the day' and 'a privileged channel for the formation and the promotion of an active laity, aware of its own role in the Church and the world'.

What more can I say? Obviously, we have felt personally touched by these theological and prophetic statements, and they are the key to understand the benevolent and open attitude he has also towards our Movement.

But there was one particular talk he gave that revealed his attitude towards our Movement and the reason for his closeness to us. It was then that he pointed out a fundamental element in the make-up of the Movement and confirmed its Marian role in the Church.

It was at the end of '86 when he came to meet seven hundred Focolarini in the present Mariapolis Centre at Castel Gandolfo. He was aware that the Focolare is a community of consecrated lay people modelled on the family of Nazareth, that is, a community of virgins with Jesus spiritually present among them, and he said that the house of Nazareth could be considered as the first Mariapolis Centre, because 'in this house, the principal mystery is certainly Christ, but Christ who comes to us through her, the woman: the woman we already hear of in Genesis, the one spoken of in the Apocalypse, the one who became a historical personality in the Virgin Mother. I think that this is part of the very nature of what you call Mariapolis, which is a means of making Mary present, an emphasizing of her presence as God himself did in the Bethlehem night and then during thirty years in Nazareth'.[53]

On another occasion when I was invited to lunch, I asked him, 'Holy Father, how do you see our Movement?' I was referring to the contribution he thought the Movement could make to the Church. His reply was, 'Ecumenism'. I think he meant it in the widest sense of the word, with regard to the Movement's openness to everyone.

Has the Movement's spirituality changed and become more updated during John Paul II's leadership of the Church?

To tell you the truth, the Pope's contribution has always been along the lines of confirming the Movement's charism, as you can see from the few extracts from his talks that we've mentioned here. His words have always been for me and for all of us a great encouragement to work so that our Movement might come more and more into its own, that is, as a creature which bears the same features as the Church, just as the Pope sees it.

I remember his firm words to me when I was kneeling before him in front of St Peter's and I was presenting the youth of the Genfest who thronged the Square. He said, 'Be always the instrument of the Holy Spirit!' These words were stamped within me, and they have reinforced in me both the fear of God and the courage to trust in the charism and to persevere on our spiritual way.

Naturally, the Pope's tremendous magisterial gifts, his teaching and his pastoral activities are all a source of light and encouragement for us. I mean for all of us but in a particular way for the young people, the Gen, the new generation of our Movement.

They have always felt encouraged and spurred on by all the talks he has addressed to young people who undoubtedly have a special place in his heart. In a letter to young people throughout the world for the International Year of Youth, he wrote: 'The future depends on you. The end of this millenium and the start of the new one depends on you. Do not be passive. Take up your responsibilities in all the fields which are open to you in our world!', a world which needs 'a profound spiritual resurrection'.[54]

Our Gen had understood the firm trust the Pope places in them, had understood that his is a youthful heart, unshakable by the current trend of pessimism, when they declared him as their leader.

Our young people, and this is a good sign for the future, recognize that their way of life is in tune with the Pope's teaching. On several occasions, they have seen that when they adopt as their own even just one of the desires he expresses, their own unity becomes truer, more universal and more practical.

IX

Women in the Church

The President Will Always Be a Woman

You were an observer at the extraordinary Synod which marked the twentieth anniversary of the Second Vatican Council and at the Synod of the Laity. You were also nominated as a consultant for the Council of the Laity. This brings me to the significance of a feminine presence in the Church. Is the narrow attitude that the hierarchy has always had with regard to women at higher ecclesiastical levels changing and, if so, in what way?

What counts more than a statement of principles is the actual practice of the Church and, in my opinion, this is where you can see signs of what you might call shifting tendencies.

I'd like to tell you of just one incident which I think is quite important and which concerns me directly. John Paul II knows our Movement, which is made up of lay people in various forms of consecration, young people, families, people committed in the world, priests, men and women religious and, on several occasions, he has emphasized the Movement's strong Marian features. Since it was our hope that in years to come, the Movement might retain its Marian identity, not only at a spiritual level but also in its public profile, thereby preserving God's plan for it inasmuch as he entrusted its conception and development to a woman, one day I plucked up courage and asked him confidentially if he thought it possible to have it confirmed in our statutes that the president of the Movement should always be a woman. He replied with enthusiasm, 'And why not? On the contrary!'

Now revised and officially approved by the Holy See, our statutes contain this clause, which represents perhaps an innovation, at least with regard to the new movements in the Church. The statutes provide for a woman, although she does not have Holy Orders, to preside as the head of a Church movement whose membership includes, in addition to the laity, a strong representation of priests, men and women religious, as well as a good number of bishops who share the spirituality of the Movement.

All of this indicates, I think, new horizons for the role of women in the Church.

There is Priesthood and Priesthood

What do you think of the ordination of women?

This is still a burning issue especially because of its ecumenical implications, for example, in relations with the Anglican Communion. First of all, I would like to say that women bring to the ecclesial framework values that are fundamental and indispensable and that, in God's plan, their place in the Church is to defend these values, which are inherent to their specific vocation.

Yes, it's true that Jesus did not speak on this subject, but he gave his incomparable model to female humanity, the one to whom all the great Christian women in history have looked, and that person is Mary, his Mother. Every woman who truly wants to serve the Church can recognize her calling by looking at Mary.

By discarding all the false and exploitative images of Mary and by looking at Mary herself, the Christian woman understands that it is not the priesthood she should be aiming at, since in the wake of the Mother of God, her role in the Church is another one, which is both important and indispensable. She must affirm, in the way in which only she can, the value and primacy of love compared to all other gifts, compared to all other elements that go to make up our religion, including the very high honour conferred on those who are called to the priesthood.

Yes, love is more important. We know it well. You do not go to heaven because you are a priest or a bishop. You go there because you have loved. While priests and bishops are the pillars on which Christ has placed his Church, they can also find themselves in hell. In that place you will find neither women nor men who have loved.

Love is the most important thing. Even the fact that the hierarchy and the sacraments themselves are only for this earth tells us that what endures into the next life is love. A part of God's people must affirm this truth leaving no room for any misconception.

It is through supernatural love, and for love and with love that a woman—whose very being is already fashioned with that natural love that makes her capable of every sacrifice—can find her own place in the Church. Minister of love as indeed she is, womankind continues throughout the centuries as she does today, to keep Mary's presence alive in the Church. This ministry of love makes the work of the priests and bishops more fruitful and reminds them of what Paul said about the vanity of giving your body to the flames without charity. It follows, therefore, that being a minister of God without love is not in accordance with God's will and that where there is no love, everything is reduced to an outward form, to mere ritual.

And so even if 'they are not called to the priesthood', as the Pope said, and 'the teaching of the Church on this point is very clear, this in no way alters the fact that women are very much an essential part of the evangelical plan of proclaiming "the Good News of the Kingdom" '.[55]

And they can carry out this charge especially through that greatest of charisms, the charism of charity. The Pope also said: 'Just as it is true that the Church at a hierarchical level is guided by the successors of the apostles and therefore by men, it is even truer that in a charismatic sense, it is women as well as men who guide it, and perhaps even more so'.[56]

It was the Pope who also confirmed the theologian, Hans Urs von Balthasar's assertion that 'Mary is Queen of the apostles without claiming apostolic powers for herself. She has others and more of them'.[57]

When women fully live out their vocation with faith and nobility and love for Mary, they reveal to the Church 'the Marian dimension in the life of Christ's apostles', and it is through this that the Marian profile, which is vital to the Church, can be kept alive and portrayed.

Re-Humanizing the Structures

You took part in a meeting of Superior Generals. How did you feel as a lay person and a woman in such a male assembly?

It was all very simple. As had been requested, I shared my spiritual experience, which is really the story of the Movement. I answered their questions with the greatest of ease, because it was just a matter of telling them about something I had lived. I think that because they were all superiors of religious orders and congregations, they had a special sensitivity regarding the charisms of the Church.

How important do you think women are in Christian spirituality today, in everyday life and in the life of society?

From my travels and meetings with people and different groups in the various continents, it seems to me that a new type of woman is emerging. You come across these women in the Movements and organizations, in the new religious families and groups formed before and during the Council, both in Italy and abroad, all different faces of the Church in which you have to recognize the work of the Holy Spirit. You find these women in every environment: in family life, in workplaces, in schools, in hospitals, in Church structures, and they are virgins, married women, mothers, young people and adults.

The spiritualities of these new Church organizations, or at least some of them, have certain elements in common, which are particularly attractive to women. Men and women from all social backgrounds and vocations are drawn to them, but particularly lay people and especially women.

These spiritualities have a Marian background to them, which women identify with. They emphasize the Word of God as something which should not only be proclaimed but incorporated into one's life and lived as Mary, the Mother of Jesus lived it, keeping it in her heart as she did, in a way of life that was more a living of the Word than a preaching of it.

These spiritualities give rise to communities that are small or large-scale examples of how God's extensive family should live, where you can see the marvellous effects of the unifying qualities women possess.

Women such as these are well-aware of the efforts being made to secure women's rights, and they are committed to working for them where appropriate. They know that much has yet to be done, but they do not get all worked up about it. While cultures still exist in which women are nothing other than slaves, so that work for change must go on, they consider this sort of activity alone as an inadequate means of securing full happiness and fulfilment for women. Their main hope lies elsewhere. It is in unity with Jesus who is love incarnate that they see a more potent means to this end. They live his message in a new way, and they are in tune with the needs of the Church today. They believe whole-heartedly in a God of love and are frequently drawn to return his love by loving him in others. Of course, women do not have a monopoly on this love, but they are particularly predisposed to it, and their response is accompanied by all the attributes of their femininity.

Regarding family life, this new kind of woman makes every effort to maintain the presence of Jesus in family life. The new awareness which exists now of the dignity and equality between men and women, also within a marriage, provides a basis for relationships in which an attitude of continuous self-giving enables every member of the family to live for the others and to find ways of sorting out difficulties and conflicts. A capacity to forgive others and a sharing of the tasks and responsibilities within the family allows the family to enjoy a new sense of peace and opens it up to the world outside.

This is the attitude these women bring to society at every level. This reaching out towards the other, this sensitivity to the needs of each human being is a female characteristic that brings a sense of urgency, of vital energy, and a more humane dimension to the whole spectrum of human activity. These women are involved with the problems of humanity, and this is why they work for a more just distribution of wealth and the means of survival. This is why they promote international solidarity and why they are able to recognize the eventual future potential of even the smallest efforts to provide solutions. This, too, is why they are concerned with the environmental problems the world faces today.

This new type of woman understands that the story of the human race is a slow and laborious unfolding of universal kinship in Christ. This woman works to create this understanding at every level. The love she has in her heart is a universal one and embraces everyone without discrimination or preference.

Yes, I am convinced, perhaps also because I can already see numberless examples of this type of woman, that at the heart of the Church, a new woman is emerging who perfectly fulfils her femininity.

The Imitation of Mary

Are your views exactly the same as those expressed by John Paul II in Mulieris Dignitatem?

Apart from the Gospel, no other document throughout history has done as much to celebrate women's dignity.

I share the Pope's vision of women as he presents it in *Mulieris Dignitatem*. I would like to make a few comments and recall some passages which particularly impressed me where you see a new vision that contains hope for the future and a greater recognition of women's dignity and their role in both secular and religious spheres.

With remarkable perception, the Pope points out the significance of women within God's plan throughout history and within the unity into which the whole of humankind is called. He places his emphasis on those truly fundamental values which nip in the bud all possible discrimination towards women and, in doing so, he restores splendour to God's work of creation.

The Holy Father makes the connection between Mary and all other women in his outline of the fascinating role played by Mary the Woman throughout the entire history of salvation.

But don't you think Mary is a rather distant model and almost impossible to imitate?

We have to grow into Mary. She is how we should become and, while we know we should imitate her and live as she did, we also know how far away we are from her, the Immaculate. Here too, the document helps us to shorten that distance between us and her and shows us that while Mary is certainly to be imitated by both men and women alike, she is the ideal model for women in a particular way, in that God's plan for humankind was completely fulfilled in her as a woman. Her achievement did not deny her femininity but rather embraced it.

In that document, the Pope considers the meaning of maternity and virginity. He speaks about both of them at length and how they co-exist in a special way in the person of Mary, Virgin and Mother. He sees maternity, the actual physical condition of carrying a child, as the reason why women are inclined to reach out to others. It's not the same for men, because they do not have this experience. It explains the way women approach human relationships and the way they deal with situations. Women are especially gifted at loving others in a practical way. You could say that God made them for this.

What the Pope says about virginity is marvellous. He explains its true significance in that virginity cannot be seen merely as giving up something but more like entering into a marriage and becoming the mother of others for the sake of the kingdom of God. It is not a 'no'. On the contrary, it's an unconditional 'yes', in the complete giving of oneself to the Beloved, to God. It is love responding to love.

Is there something in Mulieris Dignitatem *that particularly impressed you?*

One of the chapters I find fascinating is the one that deals with Jesus' relationships with women. The Pope manages to show how Jesus related to and spoke with women of his time, and it seems to me to be particularly

150

relevant and appropriate for today. Jesus talked to women about the mysteries of the kingdom of God and about other profound things. Even with women who were known to be sinners, his manner was so spontaneous and straightforward that even the apostles were surprised at him. His way of treating women was unique and at variance with the practice of the day and, as the Pope points out, never do we find the least trace of discrimination in Jesus' attitude towards women but, on the contrary, both respect and honour.

For the first time in the Bible, a woman—any woman at all—is referred to as Abraham's daughter, while it was the practice of Holy Scripture to use this filial term only for men. And there were many women who followed Jesus as disciples.

Jesus' behaviour, adds the Pope, 'represents a consistent form of protest against all forms of disrespect towards women'.[58] This is very clear in his conversations with sinners. Take for example the woman caught in adultery, when Jesus exposes what today would be seen as typical male hypocrisy. The impact of truth that he embodies arouses in her accusers a sense of their own sinfulness and culpability. An incident such as this reveals the relevance of Jesus' teaching for every era.

The document strongly underlines the ability women have to understand the things of God and how they are able to enter into the heart of Christ's mystery, treading his path to Golgotha with a courage not shown by men. At Pentecost, the Spirit descends on all, both men and women. The words of the prophet are fulfilled: 'Your sons and your daughters will prophesy'.[59]

In all the situations in which we see Christ with women, what emerges is the equality of men and women.

There are more women than men in the Focolare. Does this in some way influence the way you live in the Movement?

The difference in numbers between men and women occurs in all the statistics of the Catholic Church, both in religious orders and in church attendance figures, although it is true to say that in recent years it is becoming more even. In the Focolare Movement there are more women than men, but the difference is far less than is generally the case elsewhere. However, this factor has little effect on our way of life since, while there is a great deal of communion among all, we live in separate communities and the formation of the internal members of the Movement is carried out separately for men and for women. In the light of the same spirit, both are able to develop fully their own distinctive features, which is a necessary process to reach unity in plurality and to witness to it. Our equality is not achieved through a female view of life; it's a delicate balance which is maintained by the unity in the governing body at the Centre of the Movement. The female majority in the Movement's membership is not reflected in this central co-ordinating council which represents the heart of the Movement and where, in fact, there is an equal number of men and women.

And the Future?

You had your seventieth birthday on 22 January 1990. You look wonderful for your age, but I'm curious as to whether you have thought about a successor or delegates, since it's evident that the Movement is centralized and that you repre-

sent the heart of the organization as well as being the driving force behind it.

In its two thousand years of history, the Church has always tried to safeguard the Works of God for the future. In practice this comes about through the approval of statutes which have been carefully drawn up to reflect the founding charism and to ensure that the original spirit and continuity are maintained over the centuries. I have spent most of my time during these last few months working on the final format of these statutes, until they were officially approved by the Holy See.

I would like to quote just the introduction to the statutes, which is the indispensable rule before all others, and that is 'Mutual and continuous charity, which makes unity possible and brings the presence of Jesus into the collectivity, is the foundation of every aspect of life for all the members of the Work of Mary. It is the norm of norms and takes precedence over every other rule.' As new generations come along, the future of the Movement depends on this rule being practised. It must always be Jesus among us who directs the Movement.

As to who will succeed me as president, I have started to think about it recently, but I should like this detail also to be confirmed by Jesus among us, the one who is really at the head of the Movement.

What do you reckon you have achieved in your life?

Once someone said to me, 'But how do you manage to feel responsible for so many people Chiara?' I replied, 'It's not so much that I feel responsible for people, I try to follow God.' I think I can say that I have tried to follow

153

God throughout my life. Obviously, there have been mistakes and weaknesses, and I have had to begin again leaving all that went wrong in God's mercy. My intention has always been to follow God. I have been helped in this by the community, by Jesus in our midst who has always straightened me out and got me on my feet again.

So what sort of assessment can I make? I think Jesus will be the one to do that. Has he been pleased with what I have done? I would like to hope so because the Church, his representative has approved the Movement. But even if he were to say that no, he wasn't pleased, it would be fine with me. In my heart there is only immense gratitude towards him.

X

Chiara and the Others

What did the experience mean for those young girls in Trent who shared in Chiara's adventure at the dawn of the Movement? What was it that attracted those who went on to follow Chiara as Focolarini? What did they leave behind them, and what sort of spiritual revolution did they encounter?

Natalia Dallapiccola was Chiara's first companion. After some years in Trent, she moved to the central focolare in Rome. She also played an important role in the foundation of the Focolare in West Berlin in 1959, which worked to maintain contacts with East German Catholics. After the Wall was built, she set up the first women's focolare behind the Iron Curtain at the beginning of 1962, at Leipzig in Communist Germany. During the fifteen years she spent in that part of the world, she made the first contacts with Poland and Czechoslovakia, Hungary and Lithuania, and organized the Movement's first little communities in those socialist countries. Since 1976, she has been at the Centre of the Movement and is co-responsible for the spiritual formation of its members and for interfaith dialogue.

I first met Chiara in 1943 in the middle of the war. I was fifteen years old and was living in Trent. I had grown up in a little mountain village outside Trent, called Fornace. My childhood was a very happy one in a traditionally Christian family. We used to pray a lot together, although later, when we moved to Trent, work became the priority. Until I was sixteen years old I firmly believed that the loveliest thing in the world, the one thing you couldn't live without, was love. There was no sense in life without love.

Life had been quite easy for me until various incidents came along, such as the death of my father, still a young man, and then the war. I began to learn that life was serious and hard. Although I was still a student, I had to find a job and work to give some financial support to the family. I had to give up my plans and my dreams. Little by little, all the things that had given me pleasure before, such as music, nature, friendships, began to seem less important to me, until eventually everything just seemed completely black. By then, I was convinced that love didn't exist on this earth.

My mother was a little worried about my low state of spirits and, because she encouraged me, I often used to visit a little shrine just outside of Trent. I used to pray without asking for anything in particular, but slowly and gradually a thought took shape in my mind: Wait, you will see, something will happen.

Then one day when I was at confession, the priest invited me to a meeting he had organized for the following Sunday. I went along and a few minutes after I had arrived, a young girl came into the church. I didn't know who she was, but she seemed to be so absorbed in prayer that I wondered what she might have on her mind. We went into the hall and to my surprise and delight, after the priest had made a short introduction, he invited this girl to speak to the group. I can't remember exactly what she said; it's a long time ago now, but I do remember that I was interested from the first word . . . it was something like this, 'There are many beautiful

156

things on earth: flowers, stars, children. . . but more beautiful than all is love.' She went on to talk about the different kinds of love that exist, such as the love that a mother has, the love that people have for their parents, the love that a couple have for one another, and then, 'But if love is the most beautiful thing on earth, what must God who created it be like himself?'

As Chiara spoke, I was more and more impressed by what I was hearing. I felt her words were raising me up to God and, as I looked back over my past life, it seemed as if all the happy and painful events I had experienced were all held together by the golden thread of his love and, somehow, I knew that God loved me immensely. I went back home so happy. I felt like a princess. Everything seemed to have a meaning now. This immense and personal love of God had turned my life upside-down.

Doriana Zamboni, born in Trent in 1926, was at various times responsible for different focolare centres in Italy. In 1958 she opened the centre in Paris, and it was from there that she looked after the early growth of the Movement in England, Spain and Switzerland. From 1965 onwards she looked after the Focolare in Great Britain, where she played an important part in ecumenical developments. In 1972 she moved to Belgium and, as well as becoming responsible for the community there, she looked after the communities in the Netherlands, Sweden and England. From 1976, she has had special responsibility for the Volunteers branch and is also co-responsible for the New Humanity Movement.

At seventeen, my head was full of dreams, fantasies and imaginings that usually came to nothing in the end. I used to dream and hope and really believe that one day

I would discover love, which for me meant a true relationship between people, the sort of relationship where nothing is kept back and where the joy is in the giving, but so far I hadn't found it.

It was about then that I met Chiara Lubich. It was my teacher who told me about her. He said that she was someone he thought I would like, but I was a bit sceptical myself. Meeting Chiara was something incredible. There were no questions, no advice, no words of encouragement. She just told me about the discovery she herself had made, and you could see it in her, that 'God is love'.

Now, it's hard to believe, but it's quite true, that in a flash, Chiara's convictions became my convictions too, and it was as if I had suddenly found the same belief in love that she had, without any doubts or problems at all. It left me with no desire for anything else. This new faith bound me deeply to Chiara. She had opened my eyes and my heart.

Chiara offered to study with me, in fact to give me some tutoring to help me cover two years in one year, so that we could go up to university together. I hardly knew what studying was, since I wasn't at all interested in it, so her suggestion was almost unthinkable. However, I had entered a new world where the impossible became normality, and so I accepted her offer enthusiastically. Chiara had been told by others that I was a will o' the wisp person and that my studying would probably quickly come to nothing, but she reassured me right away about this. She said that it wasn't a case of depending on me but of trusting Jesus in me.

When Chiara explained to me the sentence in the Gospel that 'It's not the one who says, "Lord, Lord," who will enter the kingdom of heaven, but the one who does my Father's will', God's will for me was quite clear: it was to study. The presence of God's love among us as teacher and pupil made me feel I could fly, and so I really got down to it, and I studied very well. I hardly need to say that at the end of the year, I passed all the exams with flying colours.

The end of the war altered the plans we had made, but at that point who was thinking of anything other than sharing with one another the fullness of joy we had found? We also felt that God was calling us to leave everything else and to live together in what later came to be called a focolare.

Since then, during all the years I have lived in Italy and in other countries, and among all the people I have met of different languages, cultures and religions, I have seen over and over again that this gift from God is suited to every race and every individual. It's like a fire that destroys illusions and builds divine truths which can be assimilated into everyday life.

It's an inexhaustible mine of inspiration and innovation which brings renewal to traditional ideas and practices everywhere.

Silvana Veronesi was born in Trent in 1929. While studying at the university of Florence in 1949, she opened the focolare in Florence and set up the community there. Following this, she was responsible for the Movement in Turin, Milan, Rome, Sicily and Sardinia. In 1960 she left for the United States to start the Movement there, and the following year returned to Italy to run the Movement's first International School of formation which was based, to begin with, at Grottaferrata and then later at Loppiano, where she made an important contribution to the birth and growth of the little town there. From 1966 to 1972, she was based at the Centre of the Movement in Rome, where she had special responsibilities for all the women Focolarine throughout the world. In 1972, her responsibilities switched to the formation of the younger members of the Focolare Movement, who are known as Gen. She is currently responsible once again for the women who live in the focolares, known as Focolarine.

As a fifteen year old, dashing around in my white ankle socks with long plaits bouncing and my satchel swinging on my shoulder, I was already asking myself how it could be that people were born only to wither away 'like dried leaves in the autumn'. I was looking for something that would live on, so that I too would live on like the characters in my history books who had achieved great things.

It was then that I was invited to meet a young woman who would enable me to get to know Jesus. I had already told my religion teacher that although his classes had been interesting and I did attend Sunday mass, I did not know Jesus.

When Chiara met me, she used my pet name 'Silvanella' and right away I felt comfortable with her. We sat down on a tiny sofa, I put my school books on the floor beside me, and she started to tell me all about herself and her friends and the great adventure they were having.

She spoke about life and about what I could already see for myself, how everything comes to an end. She said that if we had three or four lives we could live them in many different ways but, since we only have one, it was worthwhile spending it well, for something lasting and worthy of our whole existence. At the end she said how she and her friends had understood that the only thing that lasts is God and that he had become the Ideal for their lives.

It was then that I felt that all the questions inside me were understood and that there was an answer for me too. It took only a moment for me to decide to choose God as my everything in life.

When I left the house I felt as if my heart was bursting with happiness. Chiara's Ideal was mine and I was going to live for it. From then on, while I always felt very closely bound to Chiara, it was a relationship with her in which I felt completely free. Together we were obeying Someone else. It was God who was gradually revealing his plans to Chiara, and she was able to make us share so much in them that we felt them to be ours too.

Graziella di Luca was born in Trent in 1925. She spent many years founding and developing various centres of the Movement, first in Italy, then in the Low Countries, Great Britain, France, Spain and the United States. She was involved at an editorial level in the magazine New City *and, from the publication's headquarters in Grottaferrata, she was responsible for its first foreign editions. Between 1969 and 1977, she was first of all co-responsible for the Gen Movement and then for the New Humanity Movement. From 1972 to 1990 she was responsible for the women Focolarine who live in community as well as the married women Focolarine. At the moment she is based at the Centre of the Movement and is co-responsible for all that concerns the Movement's witness and diffusion.*

I come from a middle class family in Trent. My father who was an ardent Marxist and theosophist was extremely gifted; a brilliant writer and designer and so on. My mother, a Catholic, was a private and industrious woman. I had three brothers. When I was twenty-two days old I was already travelling; we left Trent for Messina.

One incident when I was three is as clear to me now as if it happened yesterday. My grandma called me over to her and opened up an old cupboard from which she drew out a book with a coloured cover. On the front there was a picture of Christ. It was the Bible. I understood then that this was Someone who had something to do with me.

My mother was keen for us to practise our faith and fulfil our religious obligations, and my father respected her wishes. I must admit, however, that I had a robust aversion for all things churchy. I was more concerned with music, poetry, dancing, sport, theatre and cinema. As well as being a champion basketball player, an audition landed me a leading part in a film which I turned down because the people I had to work with offended my idea of what art was all about. At school I revelled in every subject the curriculum had to offer. I managed to succeed in everything I applied myself to without any real difficulty, and so it wasn't long before I became quite bored.

When I was twelve, I fell in love with a boy who was ten years older than me. It was platonic love. It was about then that I experienced the unusual need to go to confession. After I answered some questions he put to me, the priest suggested that I find a spiritual director. 'A spiritual what?!' I thought to myself. His suggestion had completely turned me off, but, as I left the confessional box, I was conscious of having acquired a new light, and I understood that a priest is like a bridge between your soul and God.

Soon the war broke out, and I was only seventeen. One day I was out on a walk, and I found myself thinking of all my question marks about life and its meaning. Since I didn't have any of the answers I soon felt very down-hearted. When I got to the corner of the street there was one of those little alcoves in the wall with a figure of St Francis. I stopped to look at it and mentally addressed St Francis, 'If God exists, if you are a saint, let me find some answers and help me to understand what it is that I feel I need so desperately.'

The war continued with its destruction of cities and people. Messina was devastated and we went back to Trent. I continued my search for answers. One day I was out again for a walk on my own when a man came up to me to beg for some money. I opened my rucksack and gave him my packed lunch. He took my hand and kissed it. I thought his reaction was a bit excessive since I had only done what anyone would do, but I felt a happiness inside me that I had never experienced before. It was as if something was telling me that things would have to change, such as my attitude, my life, me, but I didn't know how that was going to happen.

On 2 September, there was the first terrible bombing of Trent. I found myself with my face on the ground and my nails clawing the earth. Between one explosion and the next, during three successive raids, I was beside myself with fear. The whole of my life passed before my eyes. God existed but not in my life, which somehow seemed so empty now. Without caring who heard, I shouted with all the strength of my lungs, 'My God, my God, don't let me die now that I have understood what it means to live!'

Three soldiers arrived to move us, because some bombs had fallen nearby and, while the one that had exploded hadn't hurt us, there were others that could go off at any moment. I started shivering, realizing how close God's intervention had been.

A few days later, one of my colleagues at the office invited me to a meeting. I asked, 'Is it religious?' 'Not at all', she replied, but it clearly was religious, so I decided to tease her and said I would go, meanwhile thinking of how I would dress up in the latest style just to see how they reacted when I turned up.

The room was low and badly lit but what I did see in the corner was a statue of St Francis in a state of meditation. Could he possibly be thinking of answering me today? I wondered to myself. Then some girls came over to welcome me. They were Chiara, Natalia and Dori. They acted as if they had always known me. More unusual than that was the fact that they were also dressed quite fashionably. Chiara spoke about the love St Francis and St Catherine had for the poor. It was something which poured out of her as if she were on fire. And then something happened which is quite difficult to describe but which is as vivid to me today as if it happened yesterday. It was as if I could see a great light and I understood that it was God, but God who was infinite love. This light and this love seemed to fill me completely. I knew that the emptiness I had felt was now filled.

I had found what I had been looking for. I knew I had to respond to this love, his love, with a 'yes' that would encompass the whole of my life. I would have to become love which answered Love. The light I experienced as his presence was so strong that I knew then that I had no choice but to give myself to him completely. God had done ninety-nine per cent and what remained was for me to give my one per cent. I understood that I had to follow him right to the end, to holiness. It was extraordinary but also quite logical. It was clear that if I did not say my 'yes', then God would not call me again. There

I was, a girl who never cried because she had to be a tough woman, crying my heart out.

I got up, went over to Chiara and gave her all the money I had in my purse. 'Do you have a spiritual director?' I asked her. 'I want to make a general confession.'

It was as if I could see how everything in my life had been leading to this moment. It was then that my life, and the wonderful story which followed, really began.

Giulia Folonari is one of eight children in a family that runs a wine business. Together with her, two sisters and a brother became Focolarini.

Four of us followed Chiara. I was the eldest, then there was Vincenzo, Camilla and Bruna. I got to know the Movement in Brescia when I was twenty-four years old from Valeria, one of the first Focolarine. A few months later, three of us were on holiday in the mountains at San Martino di Castrozza. My other five brothers and sisters were still at school, and so at home with my parents. There was a group of Focolarini staying at Tonadico di Primiero, which was quite near San Martino, so we went to visit them. All three of us were impressed, but most of all my brother Vincenzo who was then twenty-one years old.

Our parents had given us a Christian upbringing, but it was Vincenzo more than any of us who felt a strong spiritual calling, although not to the priesthood. 'I just don't see myself as a priest in that long cassock', he used to say. After that meeting with the Focolarini, he shared with us what it had meant for him saying, 'I have found my way.'

And this is how it happened for me: At home in Brescia, I was often at the house of Enrico Roselli, a

Member of Parliament who spent his time between there and Rome. I had just got my degree in Business Administration and one day Roselli said to me, 'What are you doing here in Brescia? You have finished university, you don't need to earn your living, and there is a woman like Chiara Lubich around who happens to have moved to Rome. You should come.'

I made up my mind right away, but first of all there were my parents. I tried to say, 'I want to go to Rome; I have found people who live the Gospel.' My mother objected on the grounds that you can live the Gospel anywhere and you don't have to go to Rome to do it. It was my father instead who gave me a hand. 'I have got some business that needs to be done with a government department. If you go, you can get it dealt with faster.' He handed over a file of papers to me. It seemed that God was encouraging me, so I took the file and left that same morning.

I landed up in focolare on 12 September 1951. I knew it was for me. I found a job right away as a teacher in a school of commerce, and at Christmas I wrote home to say that I wouldn't be back. Dad replied immediately saying, 'We understand, stay there, but whenever you want to come back, this is always your home.'

Vincenzo too came to Rome that year to study chemistry at the university, but most of all to be near the Movement. In 1953, he entered focolare and Camilla and Bruna joined us a few years later.

When my father died, my mother who was always careful about family finance, agreed with all of us to hand over our part of the business to the boys who were at home and to share the rest of the estate among those who us who were in focolare and a married sister. Property and farm land at a place called Loppiano, about twenty kilometres from Florence, came to Vincenzo.

My brother handed this over to Chiara just at the time when she was beginning to have the idea that our spirituality, which is a collective one, should have a place where all the vocations in the Movement can be together, a city of the spirit. A trip to Loppiano made it clear that the property was ideal for such a project, so we kept it and, little by little, the first permanent Mariapolis came to life there.

The little town of Loppiano now has about five hundred residents. Many of them come from other continents to spend two years there studying and working. Others, mostly young people or families, spend a shorter time. Loppiano is a witness to a community of people whose life is governed by the Gospel.

Vincenzo died tragically one Sunday while swimming in the lake of Bracciano. That morning he had taken part in a community meeting and had come out from mass looking particularly radiant. Someone asked him to take a visitor, a boy called Gabriel, out for a run in the car. They went to the lake and hired a boat. Vincenzo dived in and hardly had time to say, 'It's freezing', and to Gabriel, 'Make for the shore and call help. . .' and then he went under. 'He was still smiling', remembers Gabriel. Vincenzo was thirty-three years old.

We feel Vincenzo very close to us. There is something that unites us deeply and, in many situations, there has been proof of this.

I have been Chiara's secretary for many years now, while Camilla is responsible for the young girls in the Movement called Gen 3, and Bruna works in the administrative offices at the Movement's centre in Rocca di

Papa. Before my dad died, he gave me his blessing. I was close to him at the time and was able to tell him why I had gone away. Mother, who, when I made my choice, used to repeat worriedly, 'But what is this Movement?' later got to know Chiara well herself and, in fact, grew very close to us all.

Enzo Maria Fondi was born in 1927. He graduated as a doctor and surgeon, and in 1950 at the age of twenty-three, he entered and formed part of the first focolare in Rome. He practised medicine for about ten years including two as assistant surgeon in the Catholic Hospital of Leipzig in Germany. In 1964, he was ordained a priest at the service of the Movement. At present, he is responsible for spiritual formation in the Movement and for interfaith dialogue.

In my last years at school I happened to read a book by Alexis Carrel called *Man, the Unknown*.[60] It gave me much inspiration for my future life. I was fascinated by the medico-biological sciences, with their insights into psychosomatic relations, that is the interaction between the body and the mind in health and illness.

However, there was the war and the Anzio landing took place just a few kilometres from my home, plunging all my family into the trauma of carpet bombing, during which we were surrounded by the military and our house destroyed.

Rome seemed safer, so we moved there with the few things we could salvage. Life began again, and I managed to get into the faculty of Medicine. During those early years in Rome the most important thing that happened to me was my meeting and subsequent involvement with a group of young people who belonged to a Marian Organization called *La Scaletta* at St Ignatius' Church.

I was undoubtedly drawn to radical witness, and that is perhaps why I accepted an invitation to preach a mission with the *Pro Civitate Christiana* in Siena's piazzas in 1948.

But all in all, those years were years of enquiry marked by a sense of expectancy, of vague dissatisfaction and even aridity. This is how I was during my fifth year of medicine when, in the February of 1949, I was invited to attend a meeting. It was there that I met Chiara, who was introduced by a friar and went on to tell of her own spiritual experience and that of the first group of people around her.

I could almost tell you word for word what I heard, not because I remember what was said then, but because it is 'the story of the Movement', which since then I myself have told on countless occasions as if it were my own personal story. It was the simple, calm account of events that had happened; marvellous and exceptional events and yet, at the same time, quite ordinary. It was a matter of accepting or rejecting the story. If you accepted it, there was no other way to find out more other than by following that young woman who (and you could see it for yourself) was herself the living experience, in that she genuinely embodied the story she told.

The deciding event for me was the trip to Trent during the Christmas holidays of 1949 at the start of the Holy Year. In the town practically submerged in snow, I found myself prevented from slipping on the ice by strong and loving arms, and made to feel at home by the kindest sort of people. I was at the heart of the new community.

But what struck through to my soul and left an indelible mark were the unforgettable meetings with Chiara in the little dining room of a chalet, halfway up the mountain, above the Franciscan church. Between visitors and locals there were about thirty of us, incredibly squashed together in the small space, but the way Chiara replied to the questions of a priest who was present made us forget both time and space. We were carried into an unknown dimension, into trinitarian love. It was pure contemplation and participation in the light which is the kingdom of God among us.

When I got back to Rome, it was hard to come down to earth and to get used again to the oddness of daily life made up of studies, family relationships and the ordinary activities of everyday existence. . . .

A few months later, on the eve of my graduation, I understood that what really mattered in my life now was to follow Jesus on this new path. I was ready to leave my family, my friends, my studies so as to live with him among us, together with others called to live in the same way and under the same roof.

We were spending one night in a vigil of prayer for some urgent need in the Movement, and we were taking turns to sleep and pray, so I took my bed over to the focolare. It turned out to be the first night of a new life.

In the first months after university, I learnt many new skills . . . in the kitchen of the focolare and in various other chores. But above all the focolare was a school of unity, where we learned to keep Jesus present among us twenty-four hours out of twenty-four and to overcome that deep-rooted inability to love which afflicts us all.

It is a school that continues with exams that are never over. But the secret of this life is all in the love with which God loves us and with which we, always starting again, try to love one another.

Oreste Basso was born in Florence in 1922. He graduated as an industrial engineer and was director of Breda's electro-

mechanic and locomotive departments and assistant to the Professor at the motor construction department of the Polytechnic of Milan. In 1950 he was involved in the setting up of the focolare and community in Milan. In 1953, he opened the focolare in Parma, which subsequently became the focal point for the spreading of the Movement in Emilia and Romagna, while continuing to work in the engineering industry until 1956 when he became responsible for the zone of Florence. In 1959, he moved to the Centre of the Movement and assumed special responsibility for the men Focolarini until 1967 when he was put in charge of other tasks. He has accompanied Chiara on many of her visits to the Movement in Europe and in other continents. In 1981, he completed theological studies at the Pontifical Gregorian University and was ordained priest for the needs of the Movement. At present he is a consultant at the Centre of the Movement.

I was born and grew up in Florence. Immediately after the war, I did my engineering degree in Pisa and found work in a company in Milan at Sesto San Giovanni. Lodging at the same hostel as myself were several other young professionals who later became involved in the Movement. We used to linger on in the dining room in the evening discussing technology, science, music and literature. One day, one of them said he would like me to get to know about something that was both interesting and attractive. It was to do with the living out of the Gospel. That's how I got to know Ginetta Calliari, one of Chiara's first companions. Her manner was simple and unassuming, but I was completely fascinated by what she said and the sort of life she proposed.

This meeting was a major turning point for me. I saw the Gospel in a completely different light. Although I was a practising Christian, I didn't know, in fact, didn't believe, that you could actually live the Gospel. I thought that the Gospel was something you listened to, or at the most, something you could meditate on, but never that it could be lived out at all times, in all situations.

When we exchanged our views about this meeting we found we were all in agreement. It was possible actually to live today just as in the times of Jesus and, moreover, like Peter, John and Andrew, we could have Jesus among us.

Ginetta came back to visit us several times. The tables around her in the hostel dining room moved closer and closer together and group after group started up. When the restaurant closed, we would cluster together on the street or in the trams. But more important than our conversations and comments was the fact that we had understood that it was about living. Month by month we tried to live out the particular sentence from the Gospel that Chiara proposed for all of us to live together. I remember one month in particular. The sentence we were living was: 'Behold, the handmaid of the Lord; let it be to me according to your word.' (Luke 1:38) It was a continuous discovery of the many splendid facets of God's will, living in love as Mary had done. That particular sentence spoke volumes to us, as did many others.

We started writing to Chiara, asking her to tell us how to go about living this Ideal. When Chiara wrote back to us she always offered new ideas, new lights to help us progress on the path we had begun.

The acid test for me was my workplace. I was in charge of three departments in my company which meant responsibility for three hundred employees. I tried to look at the workers and my colleagues through new eyes. There was Jesus to be loved in the weary expression and complaints of the man who had spent thirty years fixing bolts on to engine cylinders. It was the same with the very strict boss, who was a communist, a former partisan commander, a man who could read people, excellent as an engineer and as a member of a team.

One evening, Ginetta talked to us about Jesus crucified and forsaken. I can still recall the corner of the room where we had gathered around her. It was then that I discovered the great secret, the pure love, the key at the heart of this Ideal we had been given. I remember experiencing a joy I had never known before. It was something from heaven.

We decided to visit Trent to meet the people who had first started living in this new way. The Focolarine who had been living in five different focolares had come together to this one centre we visited, and we were also able to visit the men's focolare and meet the first Focolarini.

We spent the day together in such an atmosphere of joy and purity that we would have liked to have stayed there for ever.

Back in Milan, our desire to share that same lifestyle grew stronger and deeper. Three of us decided to move out of our separate rooms and to go and live together in a little flat. None of us as yet had ever heard the word 'focolare'. We just wanted to live the way we had seen them living in Trent. We gave away all our things to the poor, so that we would only have what was really necessary.

I got to know Chiara in Florence. I remember we were standing under a little archway alongside the River Arno, and she asked me to tell her about myself, about my life. I can't remember exactly what I said, but I do remember how simple and yet deep and joyful that meeting with her was. It was as if she had always known me and, somehow within me, I knew that Jesus had looked upon me and that he loved me and was calling me.

That year, it was the Christmas of 1950, Chiara invited to Rome not only the Focolarini but also some who were likely to become Focolarini, including me. There were fifty or so of us in all and the days we spent together were filled with communion and joy and light. I was won over for good by the idea of always being able to live with Jesus in the midst.

That Christmas marked my entry into focolare in a real way, in that I also left my own family to join this new family to which God was calling me.

Aldo Stedile was born in 1925. His home was in a mountain valley near Rovereto, Trent, where he attended secondary school. After the war, he worked as a painter in Merano, Bressanone, in Trent and from home. Shortly after meeting the Movement in 1948, he joined Marco Tecilla and Carlo Cimadomo to open the first men's focolare in Trent. In 1952, he moved to Rome to study theology at the Pontifical Gregorian University. March 1958 found him in Belgium, where the Movement had been invited to begin working. From Belgium he went to Germany and, in time, focolares were opened in Cologne, Munich and Heidelberg. During this same period he also began the Movement's work in Switzerland and Austria. The Movement's ecumenical activity began in 1960, and he moved to Ottmaring near Augsburg in Germany, which was to become the base for the little ecumenical town which was founded in 1968. He remained at Ottmaring for a

further sixteen years, during which time he was co-responsi-
ble for the life and activities of this ecumenical foundation. In
1963, he was ordained priest. After serving in a variety of
roles at the Centre of the Movement, he now has special
responsibility for the branch of the Volunteers.

After secondary school, I wanted to attend the Academy
of Fine Arts and study painting. With the War barely
over, this proved to be almost impossible. Instead, I
started working to earn some money, so as to be able to
finance Art School. Some portraiture, some ornamental
work and restoration I managed to acquire here and
there increased my passion for art. People convinced me
that I was good and that I would have a future as an
artist, so I was both pleased and hopeful about my
future prospects.

It was 1948 and I was twenty-three years old and
courting a lovely girl. We began to plan our future and
the family we would build together. It was the custom
where we lived to follow a course of marriage preparation, so I arranged a series of Saturdays when I would
go along to a Capuchin friar for the necessary conversations.

His name was Father Onorato, and he went to a great
deal of trouble to prepare these conversations well. At the
end of our session, he used to walk with me into the
garden of the friary and tell me about a new and marvellous group which had sprung up in Trent and which
consisted of some young girls who had left everything to
follow God and put his Word into practice. They lived a
life of love, trying to see Jesus in every person they met.
Every time I went for my preparation, Father Onorato
would end our meeting by telling me something more
about this group and, little by little, his enthusiasm began

to make me feel uneasy. I began to feel a sort of conflict inside me. My love for art and my plan to build a family were now overshadowed by a choice which appeared much more generous and all-embracing. So, on one hand there were my own plans and, on the other, a way of life that conjured up a picture of the adventure Jesus and his disciples lived together two thousand years ago. To begin with, I told myself that it was really just something a group of girls had decided to do, but it wasn't long before I heard that a boy called Marco Tecilla had left his family and joined them to live this divine adventure with Chiara Lubich, the girl who had set off the first spark.

I wanted to meet Chiara. I had to admit that my future plans were not as clear as they had been before. I had to make some decisions. Carlo Cimadomo from Rovereto came with me to Trent and, when I met Chiara, all my doubts just disappeared. Bit by bit, it dawned on me that Chiara and her friends were living the sort of communion Jesus must have lived with his disciples. For her part, Chiara wanted to see whether we had really been called by God or whether it was just a temporary infatuation, and I am convinced that in that moment Jesus made her quote those words of his which truly summed up what we felt Jesus was asking from us. She said: 'Whoever wishes to follow me, let him deny himself, take up his cross and follow me.' As we left Piazza Cappuccini and Trent itself, all I could hear were those words: 'Come, follow me!'

I had seen the Gospel lived out in the lives of these people; I had got to know a living Church, to which I was privileged to belong. On 1 June 1949, Marco, Carlo and I started the men's focolare in Trent. I continued my painting but with a completely different outlook now, because I had understood that for a Christian, work becomes a way to serve and to build relationships with others.

Each day I was learning so many new things from Chiara and her first companions and, as one day led into the next, the divine adventure of the Gospel, of unity, of mutual love, of the cross, continued to fascinate me more and more.

Notes

1. Luke 10:16
2. John 17:21
3. Cf. Gal. 3:28
4. Teresa of Avila, *The Way of Perfection* IV, 1; from the first handwritten editon of El Escorial, 1565.
5. Thérèse of the Child Jesus and of the Holy Face, *Autobiography of a Saint* A, no. 184; this quotation from *Gli scritti*, Rome, Postulazione generale dei carmelitani scalzi, 1970, pp. 185f.
6. Cyprian of Carthage, *De Orat. Dom.* 23; PL 4, 553.
7. Matt. 5:15-16
8. Matt. 6:28-29
9. Eccles. 1:2
10. Cf. 1 John 4:16
11. Matt. 7:46
12. John 15:12-13
13. Matt. 18:20
14. John 17:21; 13:35
15. Matt. 27:46
16. John 17:21
17. G. B. Montini, *Discorsi dell'arcivescovo di Milano 'Su la Madonna e sui santi' 1955- 1962*, Milan 1965, p. 461.
18. Luke 10:16
19. *Insegnamento di Paolo VI*, Poliglotta Vaticana 1965, II, pp. 1072-1074.
20. John Paul II, Speech at the Centre of the Focolare Movement, Rocca di Papa, Italy, 19 August 1984.
21. Matt. 22:39
22. Luke 6:31
23. Luke 6:38
24. Matt. 7:7
25. Igino Giordani, born on 24 September 1894 at Tivoli, wounded and decorated during the First World War, married, with four children, a member of the Italian Parliament, writer, journalist, after meeting Chiara worked closely with her, became the first married Focolarino, and in the Movement's ecumenical activity became the first director of *Centro Uno*. In 1974, after the death of his wife, he lived in community in the Focolare centre at Rocca di Papa, Italy, where he died on 18 April 1980.
26. Igino Giordani, *Memorie di un cristiano ingenuo*, Città Nuova, Rome 1984, p. 149.

27. Fr Pasquale Foresi (the son of Palmiro Foresi, Christian Democrat Member of the Italian Parliament) in 1950, when he was only twenty-one, was put in charge of the central Focolare in Rome. He obtained a degree in philosophy and theology from the Pontifical Gregorian University, and went on to complete his doctorate at the Lateran University. He has published several books of theology and philosophy.

28. Agostino Favale, *Movimenti ecclesiali contemporanei*, Ed. Las, Rome 1984, pp. 202ff.

29. John 12:24 (RSV)

30. Igino Giordani, *Diary of Fire*, New City, London 1981, p.13.

31. Paul VI, *Evangelii Nuntiandi*, no. 41.

32. Focolare means hearth in Italian. It is the fireside around which the family gathers, the symbol of family warmth.

33. Jesus Castellano Cervera, O.C.D, lecturer in spiritual theology at the Teresianum in Rome, consultant to the Sacred Congregation for the Doctrine of Faith and to the Congregation for Institutes of Consecrated Life and Societies of Apostolic life.

34. First published as *Unità e Gesù abbandonato*, Città Nuova, Rome 1984; two English translations: *Why have you forsaken me?*, New City, London 1985 and *Unity and Jesus Forsaken*, New City Press, New York 1985. The following quotation is a new translation.

35. Cf. Matt. 9:37

36. Chiara Lubich, *Meditations*, New City Press, New York 1986, and New City, London 1989.

37. Acts 4:32.

38. Matt. 6:33

39. Cf. Acts 4:32

40. Luke 14:33 (RSV)

41. Focolare carries the sense of home and family life in Italian cf. note 32, above.

42. Luke 23:46

43. *Ad Gentes*, n.15

44. Cf. Matt. 7:12

45. *Gaudium et Spes*, n.38

46. At the time this interview was made the Patriarch was still Demetrios. The comment made about him, however, would also apply to his successor, Bartholomeos.

47. *Incontri con l'Oriente*, Città Nuova, Rome 1987; unpublished in English.

48. Literally, Roman Encounters.

49. *Paolo VI al Movimento dei Focolari*, Città Nuova, Rome 1978; unpublished in English.

50. *Osservatore Romano*, 20-21 August 1984, p. 5.

51. John Paul II, *Discorso ai cardinali e ai prelati della Curia Romana*, in *Osservatore Romana*, 23 December 1987.

52. John Paul II, *Discorso al II Colloquio Internazionale dei Movimenti Ecclesiali*, in *Osservatore Romano*, 2-3 March 1987.

53. John Paul II, tape recording from 28 December 1986 (The Focolare Movement's Archives).

54. John Paul II, *Lettera Apostolica ai giovani e alle giovani del mondo in occasione dell'anno internazionale della gioventù* (Apostolic Letter to the Young People of the World on the Occasion of International Year of Youth), 31 March 1985, Piglotta Vaticana 1985, p. 4; 62-63.

55. John Paul II, *Discourse to the Bishops of the United States of America* (Los Angeles), 16 September 1987, in *Insegnamenti di Giovanni Paolo II X*, 1987, Libreria Editrice Vaticana, 1988: 566.

56. John Paul II, To the Youth, Paris, 1st June 1980, in *Insegnamenti di Giovanni Paolo II*, III/I 1990, Libreria Editrice Vaticana, 1980: 1628.

57. *Mulieris Dignitatem*, no. 27, note 55.

58. *Mulieris Dignitatem*, no.15.

59. Acts 2:17; cf. Joel 2:28

60. Original title in Italian: *L'uomo, lo sconosciuto*.